Five-Star Basketball Presents

My Favorite Moves

Shooting Like the Stars

Featuring
Chamique Holdsclaw and Tina Thompson
with Coco Miller, Nikki McCray, Ukari Figgs and
Stephanie McCarty

D1367917

Wish Publishing
Terre Haute, Indiana
www.wishpublishing.com

My Favorite Moves: Shooting Like the Stars © 2003

LCCN: 2002109909

Edited by Matt Masiero and Leigh Klein
Editorial assistance provided by Natalie Chambers
Proofread by Heather Lowhorn
Cover designed by Phil Velikan
Cover photography: Chamique Holdsclaw by AP/Wide World Photos, Tina Thompson by Frank McGrath
Interior photography:
Five-Star camp photography by Justin Gracenin. Photos of Chamique Holdsclaw and Ukari Figgs by AP/Wide World Photos. Photos of Tina Thompson, Stephanie McCarty, Coco Miller and Nikki McCray by Frank McGrath.

Printed in the United States of America
10 9 8 7 6 5 4 3 2 1

Published in the United States by
Wish Publishing
P.O. Box 10337
Terre Haute, IN 47801, USA
www.wishpublishing.com

Distributed in the United States by
Cardinal Publishers Group
7301 Georgetown Road, Suite 118
Indianapolis, Indiana 46268
www.cardinalpub.com

For Our Five-Star Campers, Past and Present

Foreword by Richie Adubato

When you first enter the sleepy little town of Honesdale, Pennsylvania, it's hard to imagine that in the middle of this bucolic setting is some of the most hard-nosed and exciting basketball to be seen on an amateur level. I first started working at Five-Star when I was a young coach, barely in my twenties. It was both a thrill and a challenge to be coaching side-by-side with some of the great minds in basketball. Surpassing that, however, was the give-and-take between these coaches and the talented young players, many of whom would someday become basketball stars. At Five-Star, the best players and the finest coaches have always been assembled.

But Five-Star is more than a finishing school for future pro players — it's a basketball community. Sure the competition is keen, but part of becoming a complete player and a complete person is learning to do your best, both on and off the court. Just as veteran coaches became my mentors, players today learn from professional coaches and from more experienced players. What these young players learn, they carry with them in to the world of sports, academics, business or whatever endeavor they undertake, because of the values instilled in them through competitive sports.

While Five-Star Basketball has consistently provided a great source for talent development, there is a major difference in basketball from when I first began coaching. Because of the hard work of the pioneer players such as Carol Blazejowski, Anne Donovan and Ann Meyers, young women are picking up the round ball and honing their skills with the same fervor that only young men once did. Today, young female players have a professional league to inspire them, role models to emulate and places like Five-Star to give them to the instruction and competition to raise their games. How can young players recreate this awesome experience anytime? This compilation of inspiration and instructional materials will provide a young player with both the backgrounds of some of their favorite WNBA players and tips on how they got to where they are.

Do you want to control the floor like Chamique Holdsclaw? Chamique is a perennial all-star and is capable of leading the WNBA in both scoring and rebounding. Can you attack the glass like Tamika Catchings? This phenomenal player has taken the league by storm, challenging every proven veteran and guided her young team to a new level. How about learning what it takes to be a consummate profession like Tina Thompson? Her clutch play comes in every area: shooting, rebounding, steals, blocks, defense — whatever her team needs to win, she will do. How about the versatility of Katie Douglas? She can play four positions on the court at any time. Her ability to penetrate and create from any spot creates mismatches and problems for any defense. Katie is a very valuable player with a great future.

Anyone can dream of greatness, hope for greatness and talk about being a great player. Those people who have the willingness to prepare themselves for greatness are destined to reach their goals. Five-Star can provide the avenue to develop and prepare; you must dig in and find the willingness to rise above any obstacle.

They say the teaching never stops at Five-Star ... and that extends well beyond the time spent on the Honesdale courts. It extends into the many years ahead for all who have shared the Five-Star experience. Good Luck!

Richie Adubato
Head Coach, New York Liberty

Table of Contents

My Favorite Moves

Shooting Like the Stars

Proper technique and hours of hard work are the main ingredients to successful shooting

Chamique Holdsclaw

From being selected as an AP First Team All-America for four consecutive seasons from 1996 to 1999 to competing at the 2000 Summer Olympics for the US Women in Sydney, Chamique Holdsclaw has been one of the brightest stars of women's basketball. Let's recap some of the honors Chamique has garnered during her playing career:

- Third on the all-time NCAA women's basketball career scoring list
- SEC's all-time leading scorer
- Selected as one of 12 female athletes that are inspirational role models by *Women's Sports and Fitness* in 1998
- Won the 1999 ESPY for Female Athlete of the Year
- Won the Naismith Award and was named AP Women's Basketball Player of the Year after both the 1997-98 and 1998-99 seasons

---

Five-Star Quick Hitter

We affectionately call Chamique "Spinderella." She spins with the best, and then goes right into the pull-up jump shot. To practice these skills, use the following Five-Star drills:

- Shooting Series, page 23
- Crazy Eights, page 24-25

- ◆ Averaged 20.4 ppg, 8.8 rpg and 2.6 apg in her four-year career at the University of Tennessee
- ◆ Member of three consecutive National Championship teams with Tennessee from 1996 to 1998
- ◆ In 1999, was named to the Kodak 25th Anniversary Team and designated "National Women's Player of the Year" by *Women's Basketball Journal*, *Sports Illustrated* and *Sporting News*
- ◆ In 1999 was the first women's college player to win the prestigious Sullivan Award
- ◆ The 1999 WNBA Rookie of the Year

Chamique's talent and work ethic have obviously impressed coaches, journalists and fans. Her teammates and rivals on the court are also wowed by her. "Chamique is a great one-on-one player. She has the ability to take over a game," says Kelly Miller. "Her ability to create off the dribble is a tremendous strength," says Kristin Folkl. "She is difficult to defend because she has both a strong inside and outside game."

> Chamique is a smooth player. She can penetrate and shoot the 15-foot jumper and can post at her size. She's amazingly versatile.
> – Nikki McCray

"Chamique's ability to attack the baseline is her greatest strength," asserts Tamika Catchings. "She's always been a great offensive threat because she takes what the defense gives her, and she's great at creating along the baseline. 'Mique hates to lose and is willing to put the whole team on her back so that her team can win. Some may call this selfish, but when you want to win, you have to do certain things."

"She revolutionized the game at her position," states Tina Thompson. "Chamique's 6'2" with extreme versatility. She can handle the ball well, and because of her height advantage on the wing, she can post off smaller guards." According to

Five-Star Quick Hitter

We also love to see Chamique's patented behind-the-back dribble into the lane move. To develop the behind the back dribble look at the following Five-Star drills:

♦ Ballhandling/Dribbling/Shooting Drills, page 17-18
♦ Dribbling/Conditioning Series, page 21-22

Nykesha Sales, "She has very long arms and great versatility. Great spin and fade-away moves ... she is the go-to player that any team can count on."

Chamique herself thinks that her greatest strength is her ability to create her own shot. "That's come from playing with guys and working on my handle from a very young age. I've had to work the hardest to improve my shooting touch. I'm a scorer, but I work constantly on improving my form."

During the WNBA off-season, Chamique spends her time training and has a shooting coach that works with her. "Since I play on the perimeter I need to be able to post up, shoot the three, knock down shots and handle the ball. I have to be able to do a little bit of everything."

Her work ethic was inspired in part by her high school coach. "Mr. Cannizaro (now a coach at Stony Brook) was the first to challenge and push me. He recognized my talent when I didn't know it existed." She admits to also being inspired by her grandmother, as well as Michael Jordan, Scottie Pippen and Teresa Edwards.

Working hard is also what she advises any young player to do, "Put in the work. Practice often — persistence is a key to success. Keep at it no matter what."

Seven-Heaven

From the Five-Star Basketball Archives

Purpose: Improves game conditioning, ballhandling and creation of shots off the dribble.

Organization: Practice all of the following dribbling moves and execute them from both the right and left side.

1. Inside/out dribble at elbow, lay-up.

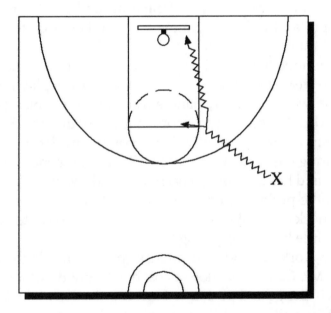

Coaches Note: If you are not making mistakes and/or turnovers, you are not going hard enough.

2.   Inside/out to crossover (cover ground) .

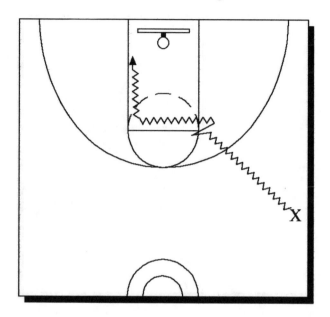

3.   Between legs to quick crossover dribble, lay-up.

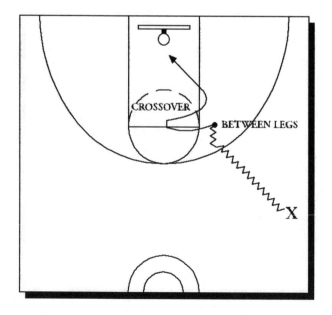

4. Hesitation, drive to lay-up.

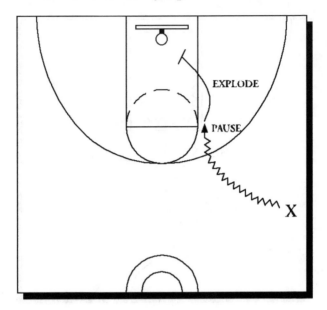

5. Spin dribble at the elbow.

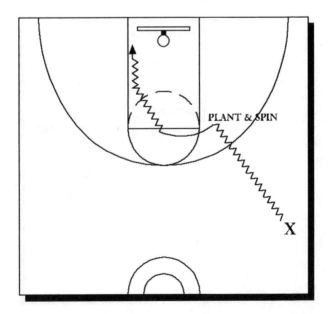

6. Inside/out into step-back jump shot.

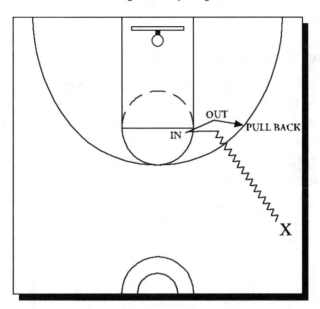

7. Spring dribble on wing into between legs at elbow, drive.

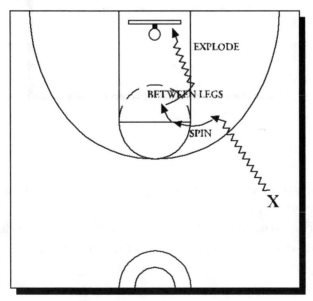

Three-Star Screening Drill

From the Five-Star Basketball Archives

Purpose: To practice catching and shooting off a screen

Organization: This drill calls for three players. Player 1 sets a screen on the first marker. When coming off the screen, player 1 gets her hands away from the defender. With her hands out in front of her, she is closer to ball and must keep low. She will then take a shot. Passer will then rotate to screener position, screener will rotate to shooter position, shooter to passer.

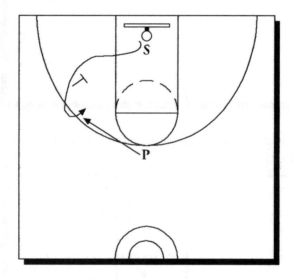

Coaching Notes: When catching the ball on the baseline facing the basket, player 1 should also practice executing a crossover and go toward the middle — this destroys the defensive rotation, which is trying to force you to the baseline.

Variations:

1. Instead of just shooting, player 1 takes two dribbles to the middle to shoot.

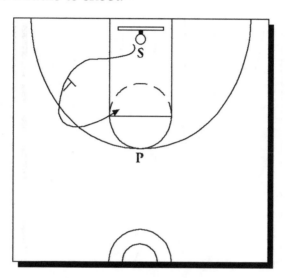

2. Instead of just shooting, player 1 reverse spins and dribbles with hand closest to sideline. She will take two hard dribbles to baseline to take a pull-up shot. This should be practiced on both sides.

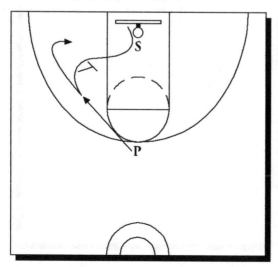

3. After coming off the screen, player 1 fades by pushing off her teammate. Pushing off her teammate's waist will automatically bring her down low.

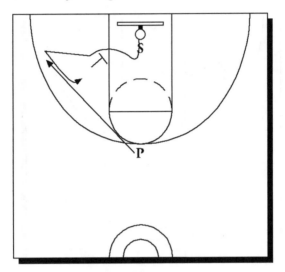

4. After coming off the screen, player 1 fades by pushing off teammate (as above) then moves to the middle with two dribbles and shoots the ball off the backboard.

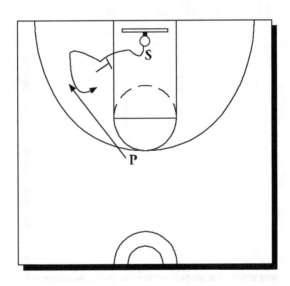

5. After coming off the screen, player 1 fades by pushing off teammate (as in variation 3), then drives to the middle with one dribble to cross toward the baseline and shoot fade.

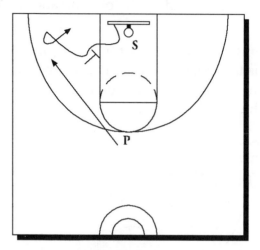

6. After coming off the screen, player 1 fades by pushing off teammate (as in variation 3), then drives to the middle with one dribble, crosses toward the baseline and shoots high off the glass to avoid the shot block. (This variation requires a shot blocker.)

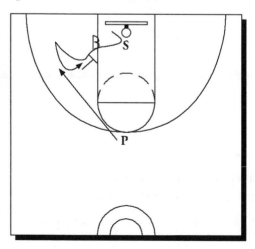

Screen Supreme

From the Five-Star Basketball Archives

Purpose: To practice reading the defense and using screens to get open.

Organization: This drill calls for three players. Player one comes off the top of a screen after faking up toward the elbow. She will then back up when she comes over the screen to catch the ball at the baseline.

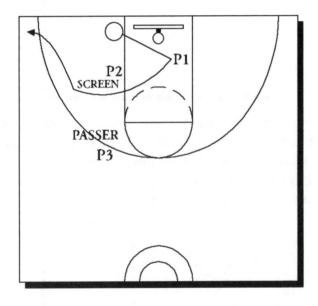

Coaching Note: It's a thinking woman's game: if you do not think the game, all of the talent and shooting will even out.

Variation:

1. When shooter comes off the screen, she will double curl into a fade toward the background.

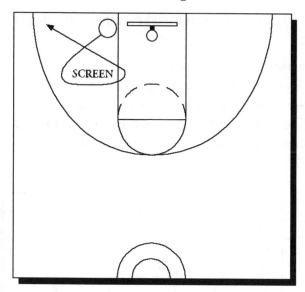

2. After shooter curls off, screener fades out.

Basketball Position Drill

From the Five-Star Basketball Archives

Purpose: To practice proper basketball positioning and shooting form.

Organization: This drill can be performed by one player. Player goes down and comes up with the ball, 1-2 step-shoot. The player must catch the ball low so that she is not only a shooter. She must catch in position to shoot, drive, pass. Practice the shot, the jab drive and the shot fake/shot.

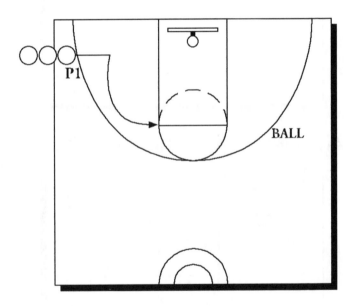

Ballhandling/Dribbling/Shooting Drills
From the Five-Star Basketball Archives

Purpose: A workout for serious players. Players may rest after each 15 seconds.

Part 1: Ballhandling	17 minutes
A. *Ball Quickness Drills*	
1. Circle Head	30 seconds
2. Circle Waist	30 seconds
3. Circle Double Leg	15 seconds
4. Circle Single Right Leg	15 seconds
5. Circle Single Left Leg	15 seconds
6. Step Back Leg	20 seconds
7. Whole Body Circle	20 seconds
8. Crab Run	30 seconds
9. Tip Front/Back	30 seconds
10. Figure 8 Dribble	30 seconds
11. Rhythm Drill	30 seconds
12. Crossover Continuous	30 seconds
13. Behind Back Continuous	30 seconds
B. *Stationary Dribbling*	
1. Inside Out Left & Right Hand	30 seconds
2. Behind Back 2 Dribbles	30 seconds
3. Behind Back 1 Dribble	30 seconds
4. Between Leg 2 Dribbles	30 seconds
5. Between Leg 1 Dribble	30 seconds
6. Between Leg 3 Dribbles	30 seconds
7. Left Hand Crossover	15 seconds
8. Right Hand Crossover	15 seconds
9. Two Dribbles Crossover	30 seconds
10. Between Legs/Crossover	30 seconds
11. Between Legs/Behind Back	30 seconds
12. Behind Back/Crossover	30 seconds

C. *Dribbling Drills*
   (take 2 free throws after each set)   5 *minutes*
   1. Step back 2 dribbles   2 sets (1 min. each)
   2. Commando Drill (execute each of these skills in succession for a total of 3 minutes).

– Inside Out	– Stutter Step
– Between Leg	– 1 Dribble
– Behind Back	– Dribble Move
– Crossover	– 1 Dribble
– Any Move/Combo	– Jumpstop, Pivot, Repeat

Part 2: Shooting

A. *70% 5-Spot Shooting*
   Make 7 out of 10 from each spot before moving on
   1. Corner
   2. Wing
   3. Top
   4. Wing
   5. Corner

B. *Shooting on the Move*
   Know the number of makes, number of attempts
   1. Elbow to corner (left side)
   2. Elbow to elbow
   3. Elbow to corner (right side)

C. *Taking Jumpers (transitional basketball)*
   Always pass on time and on target
   1. Elbow jumpers (make 10)
   2. Top/side three-point shots (make ten)

D. *One-on-One*
   Play in straight driving lines
   1. Game to five
   2. Best of five

E. *Block-to-Block—Drop Step/Lay-up*
   Coach/player hold ball on block to make player pull the ball. Player drop steps then finishes.

Post Skill Drills
From the Five-Star Basketball Archives

Purpose: To develop proper jumping and rebounding skills and improve low post shooting.

Rim Taps (3 sets)
If you cannot touch the rim, touch the backboard. Take no steps — bounce. This exercise develops your calves and is the key to jumping ability. Do 30 rim taps, 10 toe raises. Hold last toe raise for 30 seconds.

Rim Taps with Ball (3 sets)
Try to touch the ball on the rim twice before you come down to develop your hand time. Touch the backboard if you cannot touch the rim. Do 30 double touches, 10 toe raises. Hold the last one for 10 seconds.

Hook Shots (3 sets)
Shoot 10 each from both sides. Do 10 toe raises, hold the last for 10 seconds.

Laver Shots (3 sets)
Shoot 10 each from both sides. Do 10 toe raises, hold the last for 10 seconds.

Taps Drill
Tap the ball off the bottom of the board so it comes back quickly. You must quick jump — high taps give you all the time in the world. Do 10 toe raises, hold the last for 10 seconds.

Celtic Drill
Taps Drill with opposite hand touching rim (or net, backboard). Do 10 toe raises, hold the last for 10 seconds.

Power-up Drill
Bang the ball off the backboard then go back up for a shot. Do 10 each side, 10 toe raises, hold the last for 10 seconds.

Spin-Out Drill

Spin ball out to where you will get shots in the game and where you want to improve from. Make 10 shots from six different spots (60 total).

Rope Jumps

Jumping rope builds your legs and quickness. Jump one minute on both legs (forward and reverse), 2 x 30 seconds each individual leg (forward and reverse), one minute alternating feet, two minutes skipping back and forth.

Dribbling/Conditioning Series
From the Five-Star Basketball Archives

Purpose: To develop game-condition ballhandling and dribbling skills.

Game Conditioning Dribble Drill
Do the drill 2 times to the right and 2 times to the left
A. Inside-out
B. Spin (switch hands)
C. Pull back, pull back, crossover
D. Half a spin
E. Behind the back
F. Any dribble move
G. Finish

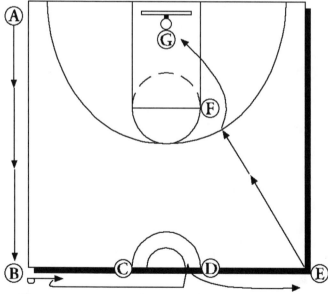

Ballhanding
Do skill A plus two others
A. Go around head, waist, knees, waist, head, etc. five times. Then go in opposite direction.

B. Zig-zag, full court dribble moves. Four times crossover, through legs, behind back, etc.
C. Do 30 dribbles each (keep feet square and head up) Right: push and pull/back and forth. Left: push and pull/back and forth. Behind the back.
D. Up two, back two (10 times).
E. Do 20 dribbling moves inside the circle.

Jump Rope
1 minute — 2 feet
30 seconds — right foot
30 seconds — left foot
1 minute — alternating
1 minute — 2 feet
1 minute — anything you want

Shooting Series

From the Five-Star Basketball Archives

Purpose: To develop shooting off a quick pass/rebound and utilize various moves.

Rapid Fire

Requires three players and two basketballs. Players shoot six shots from every "x" in group A, total 18 shots. Change shooter. Repeat drill for groups B and C. All passes to the shooter come from the paint (inside-out three-pointers).

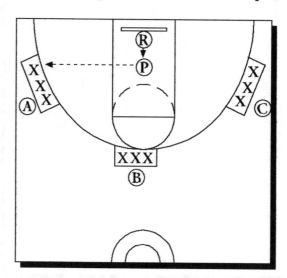

One-on-One Pull-up

Do this in the same manner as the shot coming off a screen. Spin the ball out to ANY area on the court. Catch the ball and use any of the following moves. Take one dribble and pull up. Make 15 shots.

1. Rip Through
2. Swing-Swing
3. Reverse Spin
4. Rip Through with one dribble, step back

Crazy Eights: Utilizing the Dual Dribble

From the Five-Star Basketball Archives

Purpose: To develop shooting off two dribbles while utilizing the spin and glass.

Organization:

1. Toss out, 1-2 stop, 2 dribbles, jumper.

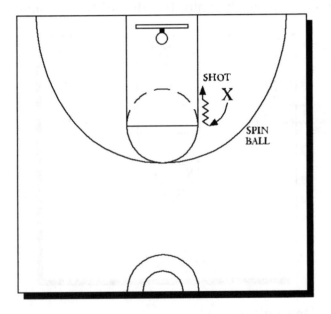

Coaching Note:

Always use the second dribble (extended) to get away from the defense.

2. Two dribbles, stutter, two dribbles around screen, back to jump shot.

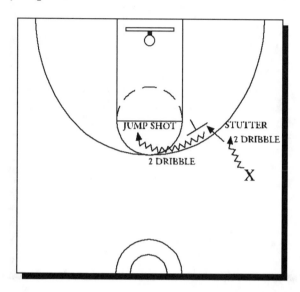

3. Two dribbles, spin, shot (spin right into shot), do not make full spin.

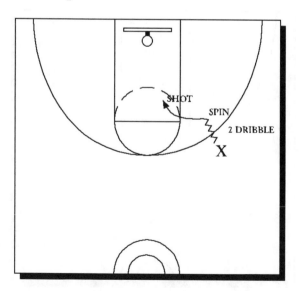

4.   Two dribbles, half-spin, shot.

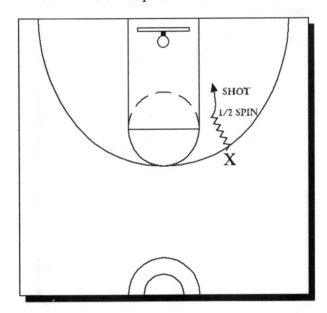

5.   Attack elbow, crossover shot.

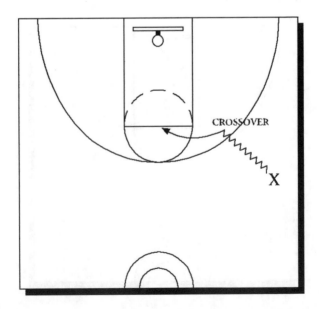

6. Straight line, stutter, dribble, shot off boards.

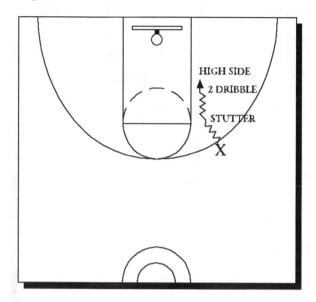

7. Runner (left and right hand) is a high jump, not a broad jump. Attack elbow, spin, runner off board.

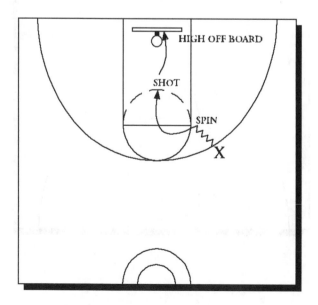

8. Attack baseline, plant, pivot toward middle, shoot high off glass. (Can also be done with half-spin.)

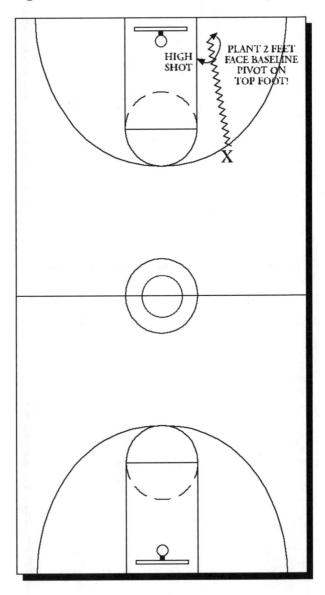

**Working on your game at Five-Star can
help you become an All-Star like Chamique**

Working hard on catching and finishing in the post will help you develop two of Tina Thompson's greatest assets

Learn to Play Like
Tina Thompson

"I think my versatility is my greatest strength — the ability to play in and out," says Tina Thompson. "I picked that up as a child when playing at the rec center. Being the only girl, I had no choice but to play with the fellas. I played outside a lot because of the strength factor and developed an outside shot and my three-point range. But because I was tall, I played in the post when I played with other girls and developed an inside game. I was able to continue working on both as I grew as a basketball player."

Her competitors agree: "Tina is a very versatile player that has great inside moves and is also a terrific outside shooter," says Coco Miller. "She can also handle the ball

---

Five-Star Quick Hitter

Like Larry Bird, Tina Thompson is the master of the step back jump shot. Her up-and-under in the post is also a force to be reckoned with. To work on these skills, we recommend watching as many high-level games as you can and working on the following skill developing regimens.

- ♦ The Post Series, pages 40-53
- ♦ Summer Program for Developing players, pages 54-59

extremely well which is rare for a post player." Nykesha Sales adds, "She's a nice scorer. Great moves inside and knows how to get it done against the taller defenders."

Tina has certainly had an illustrious career. She was Pac-10 Freshman of the Year in 1994 and finished her career at USC as the Pac-10's second leading rebounder (1168 rebounds) and third-leading scorer (2248 points). She was selected to the 1996-97 AP All-America second team, the Kodak District All-America team and the All Pac-10 first team. She was the top pick in the 1997 WNBA draft and has been a member of four WNBA championship teams with the Houston Comets (1997, 1998, 1999 and 2000).

> Tina is fierce — extremely focused and determined with a will to win.
> – Stephanie McCarty

To work on her game, Tina plays a lot of pick-up basketball "with the fellas" during the off-season. "Whether it is a fullcourt or one-on-one. I also try to shoot a lot of jumpers to improve my accuracy, as well as polish different parts of my game that need it. I think playing basketball is the best way to practice.

"The part of my game I work on the most is my ballhandling and doing things off the dribble. Because I was either in the post or shooting jump shots, I didn't handle the ball much. The more accurate I became with my jump shot," Tina explains, "the more teams and players started to force me to put the ball on the floor. I practice a lot now just shooting off the dribble and penetrating to the basket."

When asked about role models, Tina says, "My parents were my role models. They were the people that provided for me and were within reach on a daily basis. They taught me the necessities of survival, right and wrong, to respect myself as well as others. They also taught me to dream big — to set high goals ... My older brother was also influential. I followed his lead in basketball, and his sincere approach to the game and whatever else he sets his mind to was very inspirational."

Five-Star Quick Hitter

Tina is also a catch and shoot specialist using the screens. To practice this skill, use the "Jab Step Shooting Series" found on pages 37-39.

"My favorite basketball team was the Los Angeles Lakers, 'Showtime,' and my favorite players were Magic Johnson and 'Big Game' James Worthy. Not only because of the fact that they were excellent basketball players, but also because of their unbelievable love for the game and the enjoyment they found in it.

"I have a number of coaches that have been instrumental in my growth as a basketball player. But I think John Anderson has to be the most influential — he and his family opened up a new world for me through basketball. Coach Anderson is the founder of OGDL (Olympia Girls Development League), which provides young girls with the opportunity to play basketball amongst their peers in an organized environment as well as prepare for life outside of and after basketball. OGDL has a huge emphasis on college preparation, for entrance exams like the SAT and ACT and other college application requirements. I remember an incident where one of our players for our AAU team did not have an SAT or ACT study guide with her and was not allowed to get on the bus and make the trip without one. His strict and caring ways have shaped a lot of young women outside of their households ... including me. His influence is greatly appreciated."

Coach Anderson's college preparation was definitely an influence, Tina earned a degree in sociology with a minor in psychology from USC and plans to one day go back for a law degree. She clearly values education as one of the most important gifts basketball has given her, "I will always love the game of basketball as it is a passion of mine, and it helped shape me into the woman I am today — I was given numerous opportunities that I might not have had without this game. Not only has the game given me a first-class education, I have seen the world and have been able to provide my family with a comfortable living. Basketball will forever be an important part of my life.

> Winning four WNBA titles shows what kind of competitor Tina is. She's hit big shots in countless games and will do whatever it takes to win. She's also a great motivator; her teammates seem to follow her example on the floor.
>
> - *Coco Miller*

"Be passionate," Tina urges. "I always play to win, no matter the circumstances. I never step in between those lines without the intention of winning. I think that it is wonderful that there is a place for girls and young women after college basketball. That they can now have the same dreams as boys and young men. But I encourage all players not to lose sight of reality — there are only a select few that will have the opportunity to be professional basketball players. Continue to educate yourself and always a have a plan B. Love the game and play it with passion, but the reality is that it's only a game."

Pre-Season Conditioning
From the Five-Star Basketball Archives

Purpose: Develops overall footwork and footspeed, lower and upper body strength, and ballhandling skills.

Organization: Before you begin your program, find a running track and stretch before running a mile. Write down the time (goal, 6:00 minutes), put the time away and refer to it prior the opening of the season. Find hills, run in pairs. A "conversation run" should take you 15 minutes.

The following stations should be run in 1 minute increments: 30 seconds work/30 seconds rest. Your goal should be to eventually work 45 seconds and rest 15 seconds.

Station 1: Step and Slide
1. In line, step and slide. Players A and B slide diagonally up the lane and slide back to their original position.

Station 2: Full Court Dribbling
1. Dribble with the right hand up and back.
2. Dribble with the left hand up and back.
3. Crab walk with the ball forward up-court and backward down-court.
4. Charge and plant the outside foot.
5. Two ball dribble, alternate.

Station 3: Abdominal Muscles
1. Crunches with legs crossed and ben in the air, arms are crossed in the front.

Station 4: Imaginary Chair
1. Sit against the wall with back and heels pressing hard against the wall.

Station 5: Vertical Jump
1. Touch and go jumps with ball above the head. Jump and touch backboard quickly with the ball in one hand,

      tap the backboard with the ball and touch the net with the other hand.

2. Tip the ball five times with one hand. Touch the ball to to the rim and then throw it over the rim. Repeat twice.

Station 6: Stretching out Legs

1. Stationary knee to chest jumps (5 times). Then jump and kick your heels to your butt (5 times).

Station 7: Push-ups

1. Push-ups on top of two basketballs.

Station 8: Mountain Climbing

1. Push-up hands on ground, switch positions and work legs one a time.

Jab-Step Shooting Series
From the Five-Star Basketball Archives

Purpose: To improve shooting skills by utilizing proper footwork.

Part One: Jab-Step Drive
1. Player 1 starts on the right wing against the defender (X1).
2. Player 1 attacks the defender up foot with a hard right foot jab-step.
3. Player 1 then explodes with a hard drive to the basket for a lay-up. Done on both sides of the floor with both feet.

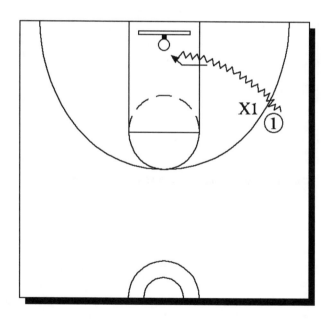

Part Two: Jab-Step Pull Back

1. Player 1 starts on the right wing against the defender (X1).
2. Player 1 attacks the defender up foot with a hard right foot jab-step.
3. Player 1 then pull backs hard for a jump shot.
4. Done on both sides of the floor with both feet.

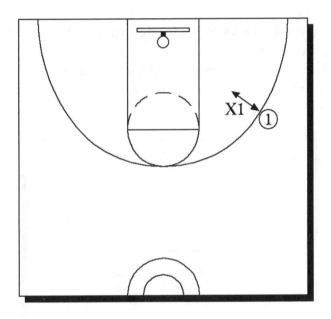

2: Drop Step, Middle

...ow wide step toward the middle of the floor. Exte...
...over ground (seal the defense). Square your shoulde...
...make a power lay-up over the front of the rim.

...ter Move 2: Pull-Back, Middle

...Begin with the same movements above, then lunge wit...
...e dribble to the middle of the lane. Swing your lead fo...
...ard the baseline, square shoulders and take a fade-awa...
...per.

Part Three: Jab-Step/1 Dribble Pull-up

1. Player 1 starts on the right wing against defender (X1).
2. Player 1 attacks the defender up foot with a hard right foot jab-step.
3. Player 1 then explodes and takes one hard dribble right for a pull-up jump shot. (The one dribble can be done either to the left or right. Do the drill on both sides of the floor and with both feet.)

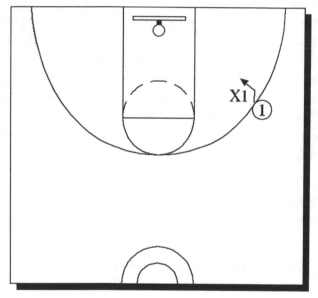

Post Series

From the Five-Star Basketball Archives

Purpose: These drill are designed to build offensive moves in the post, but skills can also be used away from the basket as well. Both post players and guards will benefit from this series.

Organization: Every base move has a counter move, which can be practiced alone or with a partner. Be sure to post above the block and begin every move with a fake in the opposite direction from which the move is intended. For example, if the move is a baseline move, start the move with a ball and head fake to the middle. All moves should begin with the player's back to the basket. The moves following are described from the right block, adjust so that you can practice from the left as well.

Move 1: Drop Step, Baseline

Long wide step on the baseline toward the basket, with a two-handed power dribble. Finish the move with a power lay-up.

Counter Move 1: Pull-Back, Baseline

Begin with the same movements as above, but lean toward the basket fake as if you were going to dribble the ball, but do not dribble. After faking the dribble, swing your lead foot (the foot you stepped with) toward the middle to square your shoulders and take a nice fade-away jumper. This can be a bank shot or over the rim.

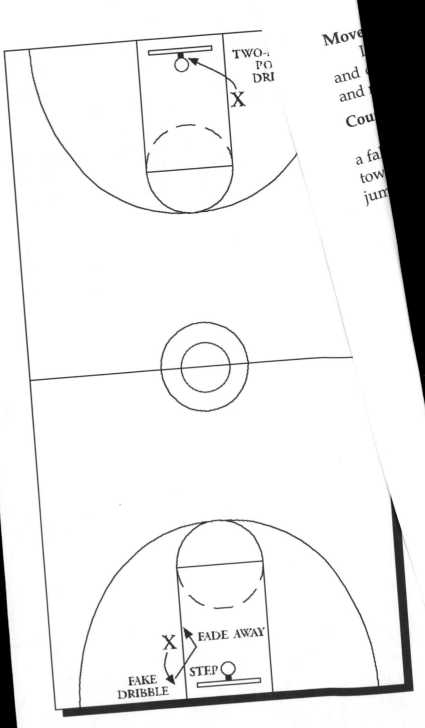

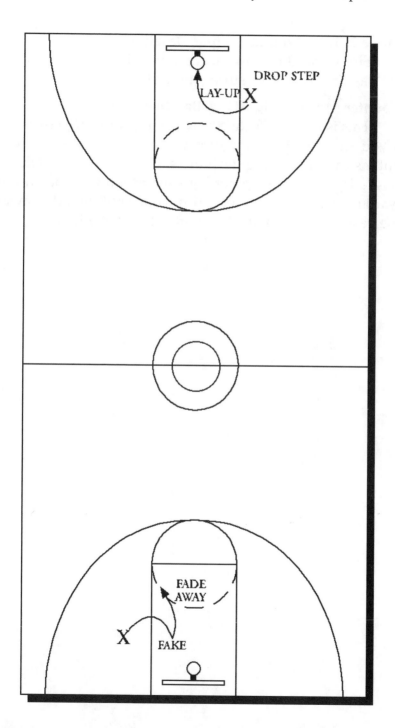

Move 3: Turn-Around Jumper, Baseline

Simple head fake toward the the middle with a pivot on the baseline leg with a strong jump shot.

Counter Move 3: High-Low, Baseline

This is a very effective move when done properly. Act as if you are going to do the turn-around jumper at the baseline but instead of shooting the jump shot, shot fake. With the opposite leg from your pivot leg, step around the defense toward the middle of the floor. Turn your right shoulder toward the basket and shoot the ball with a lefty baby-hook.

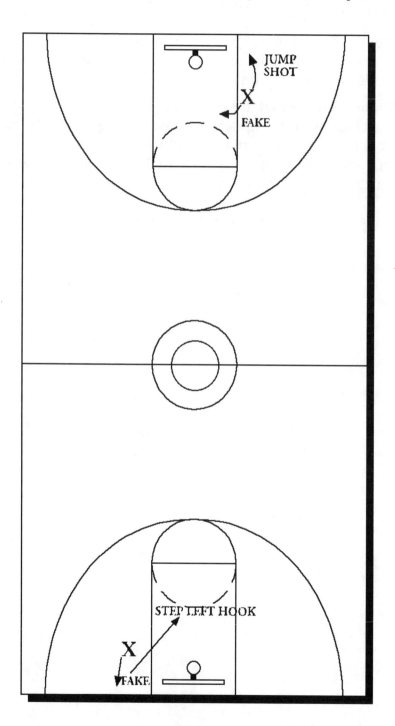

Move 4: Turn-Around Jumper, Middle

Simple head fake toward the baseline then pivot on the inside foot. Finish with a strong jump shot.

Counter Move 4: High-Low, Middle

Once again set up as if you were going to do the turn-around jumper to the middle, but instead of taking the jump shot, shot fake and step around the defense toward the baseline to extend into a strong right-handed lay-up.

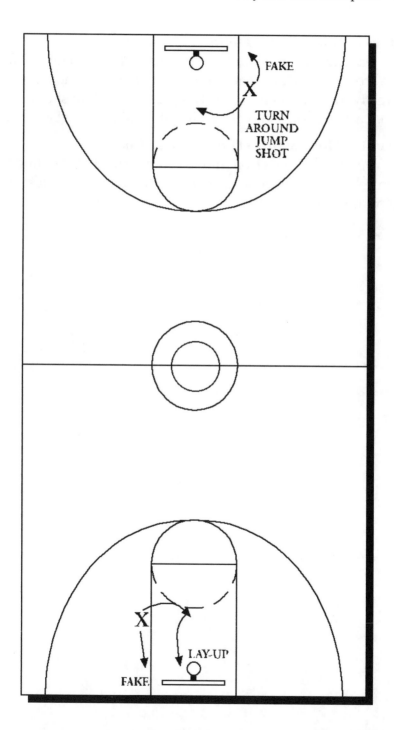

Move 5: Hook Shot, Baseline

Fake toward the middle of the floor, step with the left foot toward the baseline. The toe of your left foot should point directly to the baseline. Slightly square your right shoulder to shoot a soft hook shot with the right hand off the glass.

Counter Move 5: Step-Through, Baseline

Follow the steps from move 5, but instead of shooting the hook shot, fake the hook shot and then dip your shoulder and step under the defense.

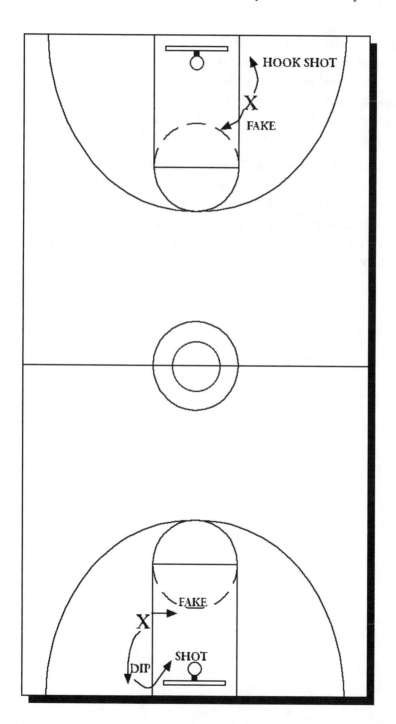

Move 6: Hook Shot, Middle

Set up on the block fake toward the baseline, then step into the lane with the right leg, pointing the toe toward the opposite sideline. Protect the ball under the chin. Square the left shoulder to the basket and shoot the hook shot with the left hand under the front of the rim.

Counter Move 6: Step-Through, Middle

Follow the steps for move 6, but instead of shooting the hook shot, fake the hook shot and dip the right shoulder under the defense and step to the basket. Depending on your positioning, this may be a finger roll over the front of the rim or a lay-up.

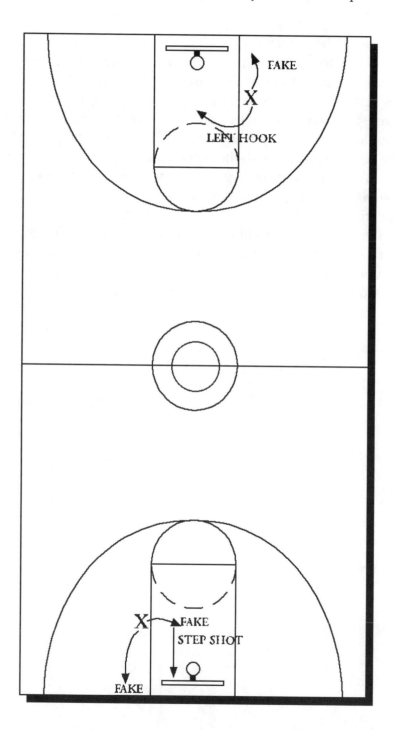

Move 7: The Reverse

Fake to the middle, turn as if you were going to take a turn-around jumper at the baseline. Shot fake. With the lead leg, take one dribble with the ball in your right hand (hand closest to the baseline) under the basket. Then dip the left shoulder, turn the right shoulder to face down court and shoot the reverse lay-up with the right hand.

All of these moves are dependent on the reaction of the defense. The counter moves are designed to catch the defense cheating after the original move has been made. Always keep the ball under your chin with your elbows out. Do not give your opponent an opportunity to reach in. Use your backside as your guide and do not be afraid of contact. The move must be strong, but the shot must finish with finesse.

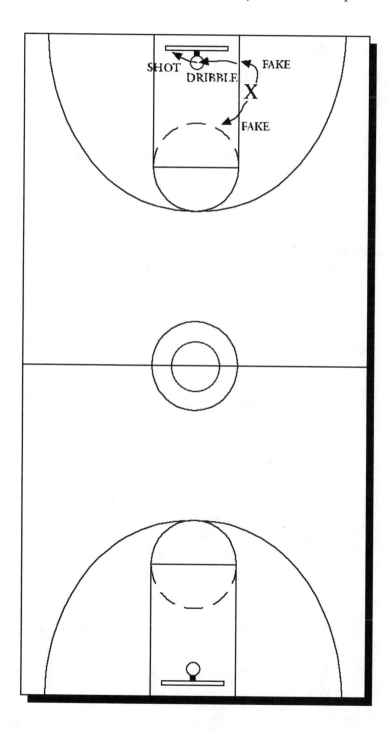

Summer Program for Developing Players

From the Five-Star Basketball Archives

Purpose: This workout will change your career if and only if you do something with it! You should work one hour a day.

Organization:

Stand in a stationary position with your knees bent and head up (parts 1-3).

Part One: Ballhandling

1. You need to be associated with the basketball.
2. You need to do these drills for your eyes and to develop confidence with the ball.

   a. Ball slaps. Pound your hand into the ball.

   b. Finger tips. Work on touch. Keep your thumbs involved!

   c. Squeezes. Ball is above the head — your forearms should get warm in this exercise.

   d. Five push-ups on two balls.

   e. Ball around. Move the ball around your head, chest, waist, knees, ankles, then go back up again.

   f. Behind back pass to other hand. This move warms up the shoulders. Keep the ball on your fingers to improve your control.

   g. Stationary figure eight dribbles. This is to develop quickness. Move your legs!

   h. Flip/flops. Flips: One hand is in front of the body, one hand is behind. Alternate so that the ball doesn't hit the floor.

   i. Toss ball in the air, clap and catch it behind your back.

   j. Toss ball from behind your back and catch it behind your head.

k. Let ball drop against your body and catch it before it hits the floor. Practice this from the waist, the knees and behind the knees.

Part Two: Dribbling

1. Figure eight dribbling with one hand.
   a. Feet are spread apart.
   b. Practice with both the right and left hands.
   c. Empty or open wrist should be "locked" and ready to protect the ball.
2. Sit down dribbling.
   a. Practice with right hand.
   b. Practice in the middle (tap with both hands).
   c. Practice with left hand.
   d. Back to middle, right dribble should be continuous. Lift legs to switch dribbling positions.
3. Crossover dribbles (at sock level). Keep your head up!
4. V Dribbles.
   a. Right hip (right hand).
   b. Right leg (right hand in front).
   c. Left hip (left hand).
   d. Left leg (left hand in front).
   e. Behind back (both hands).
5. Circle dribbles. Feet together, dribble around the body.
6. Through the legs. Walking forward and backward.

Part Three: Two-Ball Dribbling

1. Low and quick. Practice forward, backward and while changing direction. Dribble at the knee level.
2. Stationary two-ball dribbling.
   a. Circle ball in front (crossover).
   b. Stagger dribble (quicker, move feet).
   c. High dribble exchange with one hand only, use the other hand to pick up the dribble to replace the dribble hand.

Part Four: Speed Dribble

1. Speed dribble (halfcourt). Four trips: right, left, crab and two balls. Should take 50-55 seconds. Repeat five times with a 50 second break between each session.

Part Five: Agility Drills

1. Superman. Pass ball to opposite side of the glass, catch and land outside of the lane.
2. Tips. Underhand toss from the free-throw line, should be soft and above the box. Control the toss with your fingers, not your palms. Catch with either one or two hands and finish.
3. Rips. Underhand toss from the free-throw line, soft and above the box. Rip it down and go up strong and finish.
4. Rip and fake. Underhand toss from the free-throw line, soft and above the box. Make a believable fake and finish, drawing the foul.
5. Rip, fake and step across with a reverse lay-up.
6. Strong hands drill. Toss the ball up in mid-air. Catch the ball and touch the rim of the basket. Land then jump back up.
7. Quick tip. From the block, toss the ball up to the other side of the rim and tip the ball into the basket.
8. Tips and touches. As you go up to tip the ball into the basket, touch the net with the other hand. Do this 50 times and alternate between right and left sides.

Part Six: Shooting Techniques

1. Solo shooting. Shoot straight up in the air about 10 feet high.
2. Beilein shooting. Start at foul line, aim for a spot on the backboard, shoot the ball. Step back while the ball is in the air. "Load" your hands, step and shoot. Keep your hands up and in steady form

3. Beilein with shot fake. Same as above with a shot fake.
4. Beilein shooting with your body facing the sideline. Pick ball up, square up with the inside foot, push off pivot foot for a lay-up. Work with both pivot feet!
   a. Lay-up.
   b. Two dribbles, power lay-up.

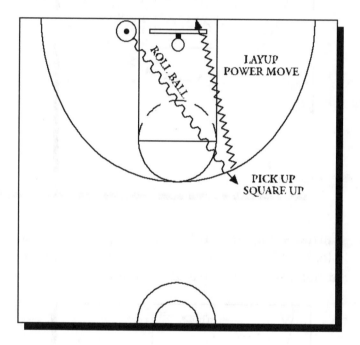

c. Two dribbles and make move: crossover, between legs, spin and behind the back (execute moves to both sides).

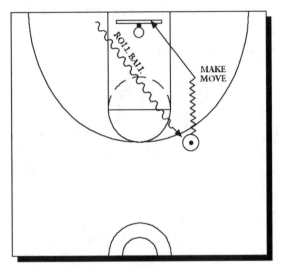

5.   Partners. Player O rolls the ball, player X slides from block to block and from has to has. Offense must dribble at defense and make a dribble move.

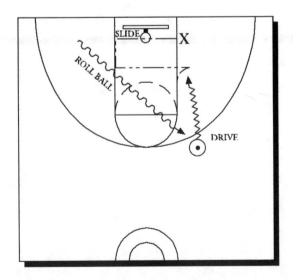

6. Block the shot. Player O rolls the ball and faces and takes the basket. Player X slides to block, to elbow and attempts to block the shot from behind.

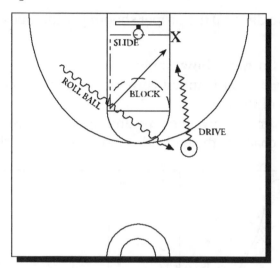

7. Friar Shooting. Roll the ball, square up and take a shot fake. One or two dribbles after the shot fake, toss ball out beyond the arc. Run behind the ball and shoot the three. Practice from both sides.

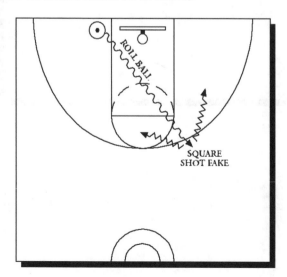

Toss Back Shooting Series

From the Five-Star Basketball Archives

Purpose: To develop the proper shooting techniques off a catch and pass.

Part One: Corner-Elbow Shots

1. Player 1 starts in left corner and passes to coach at the top of the key.
2. Player 1 follows the pass and receives a pass back from the coach at the ball side elbow for a jump shot.

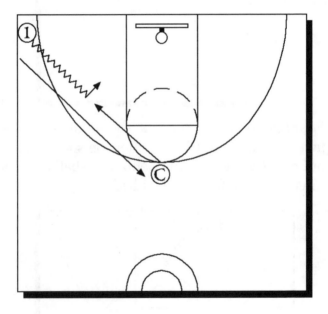

Part Two: Top-Elbow Shots

1. Player 1 starts at the top of the key and passes to coach in the corner.
2. Player 1 follows the pass and receives a pass back from the coach at the ball side elbow for a jump shot.

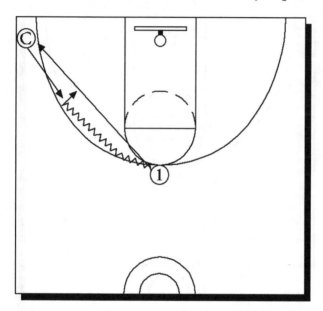

Part Three: Elbow-Elbow Shots

1. Player 1 starts at the left elbow and passes to the coach at the right elbow.
2. Player 1 follows the pass and receives a pass back from the coach at the free-throw line for a jump shot.

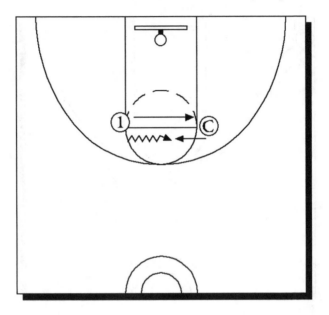

Getting low on the dribble and pulling up high for the jump shot, Coco Miller-style

Learn to Play Like
Coco Miller

"I always loved to watch Michael Jordan play when I was growing up. I would always try to imitate him and do his moves. I also loved watching my brother play basketball in

high school. He was a great athlete," says Coco Miller. "Unfortunately, not too many women's games were on television, so I never had a chance to see many women play."

Even without many female role models in the sport, Coco and her twin sister, Kelly, were encouraged to play basketball. Coco and Kelly were roommates at the University of Georgia, where they were both standouts for the

Lady Bulldogs team and students in the pre-med program. Both intend to return to school after their professional playing days are over.

"If I could let people know one thing about me as a player, I would want them to know how hard I work — and not just

---

Five-Star Quick Hitter

Coco is great with the shot fake, it's the key to her game. She also displays tremendous ball quickness. To develop these skills, give these drills a try:

- ♦ Partner Shooting, pages 65-69
- ♦ Half-Court Dribble and Make a Move, pages 72-73
- ♦ Finish the Play Series, pages 79-80

during the season and on game days. My real work begins in the off-season, when I try to improve my game," according to Coco. The off-season is anything but a break for me. I try to improve my speed and endurance by doing a combination of sprints, long distance runs and hill/mountain runs. I also lift weights four days a week, participate in basketball scrimmages three times a week and do my own basketball workout two times a week. I do all of this to prepare for the season ahead, so that I can be in top physical conditional and form. I know then that I have done everything possible to be successful."

> Coach Andy Landers had the greatest effect on me and truly helped me take my game to the next level ... He is a very intense coach, and he wants you to succeed on and off the court. His enthusiasm for the game carries over to his players and helps them be successful.
>
> *– Coco Miller*

Her hard work is noticed by those who play with her, "Coco is a perfectionist. She expects to be flawless every time she steps on the floor and that fuels her competitiveness," says Katie Douglas. Her twin Kelly says of her, "Coco is very intense and is a clutch player. She'll do anything to win, whether it's diving on the floor for a loose ball or knocking down the open jumper. She has hit many big shots in close games. Coco's great work ethic is what makes her a competitor."

"I love to run the floor and play a fast-paced game. I believe my work ethic has enabled me to achieve everything I have achieved up to now," says Coco. "My jump-shot is probably my strongest skill, but I believe moving without the basketball is the key to becoming a great player. During the season and in the off-season, I do many different shooting drills and make them very game-like, always going full speed. That way I get a conditioning and skill workout at the same time."

Coco has a variety of drills that she performs as part of her basketball workout, including the shooting drills,

Five-Star Quick Hitter

Coco's pull-up jump shot uses both her ball quickness and her shot fake. Here are some drills that will help you use both skills together:

- ♦ "T" Drill, pages 70-71
- ♦ 7 Spot Shooting, pages 65-69

ballhandling and footwork. As far as repetition of drills goes, Coco says, "I don't have a set number of shots I take per practice. I just go until my form and shot feel good."

When asked about game weaknesses, Coco says, "I don't think there was one specific area of my game that I had to drastically improve upon. Building up physical strength is one thing I've worked hard on for the last several years. I never really lifted weights until I was a senior in high school, but since I started I've noticed a difference in my game as far as speed and pure strength go. As I said, I lift four times a week during the off-season and then during the season two to three times a week. Lifting weights and keeping physically fit is now just a part of my life."

What advice would Coco offer to young players? "Hard work will take you wherever you want to go. You must be committed and make basketball a top priority in your life. You may have to make sacrifices, but if this is what you really want it will all be worth it in the end." And finally, "Practice your craft. No matter what your talent — music, sports, whatever — you must practice and want to get better. Everytime you take to the floor you should try to improve some part of your game."

Partner Shooting:
7 Shots — Shoot and Defend
Coco Miller

Purpose: Helps to develop offensive skills, especially making moves against defense. Also helps improve foot speed and develop quick reaction on defense.

Organization:
1. Begin with one offensive and one defensive player. The offensive player will take five shots from seven set spots on the floor — three spots around each wing and one at the top of the key.
2. Offensive player begins in either corner of the three point line and the baseline. For the first two shots, the defense passes the ball to offense who takes her shot. Defense has her hand up contesting the shot. For the third shot, the offensive player fakes and drives by the defensive player who plays token defense. For the last two shots, the defensive player tries to stop the offensive player from scoring.

Coaching Notes: The offense and defense alternate after each shot. Once the offensive player shoots, she gets her rebound and passes to the other player on offense.

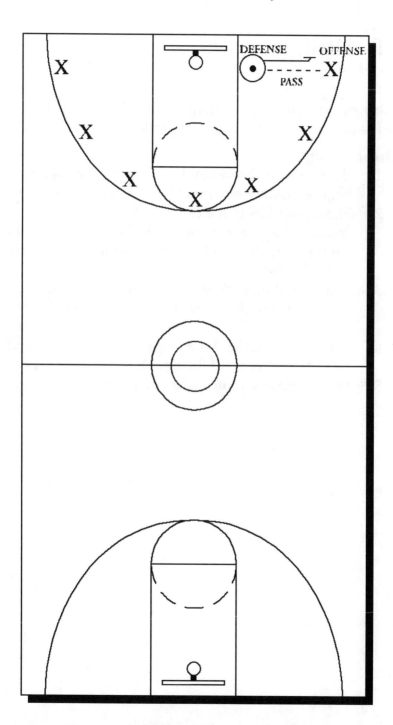

"T" Drill

Coco Miller

Purpose: Improves conditioning and shooting ability. Also helps players to remain focused while tired.

Organization:
1. Begin with a shooter and a rebounder/passer. Shooter begins on either sideline at the free-throw line extended.
2. Shooter sprints to the center of the free-throw line and receives the pass from under the basket. Shooter shoots a jump shot. Rebounder rebounds the shot and returns to the basket.
3. After the shot, shooter sprints to the opposite sideline and returns to the center of the free-throw line for the shot.
4. After the shot, the shooter sprints to half court and returns to the center of the free-throw line for a shot.
5. Drill continues until the shooter has made four round trips.

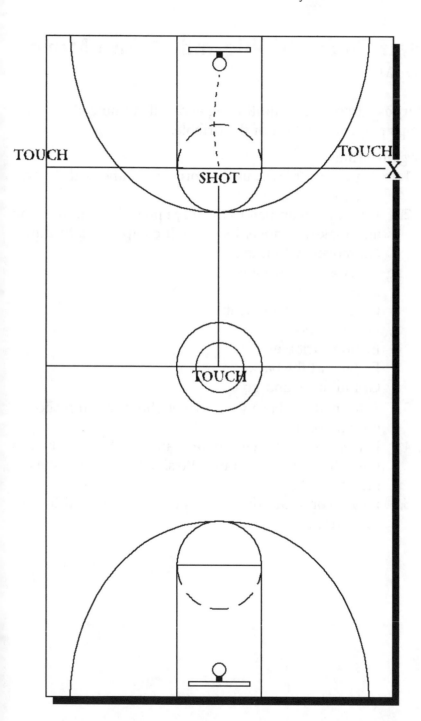

Half Court Dribble and Make a Move

Coco Miller

Purpose: Improves conditioning and ballhandling skills. Also helps players shoot off of the dribble.

Organization:
1. Begin with player in the corner on either side of half court.
2. Player dribbles ball to the three point line on the wing and makes a move. Player will complete eight different moves within this drill.
    A. Crossover dribble
    B. Stutter step
    C. Inside/outside dribble
    D. Hesitation
    E. Spin dribble
    F. Behind the back
    G. Pull back and go
3. After making her move, player shoots a jump shot or goes in for a lay-up.
4. Player gets her own rebound and dribbles the ball to the half-court on the opposite side from which she began the drill.
5. Player continues drill until she has completed four of each move.

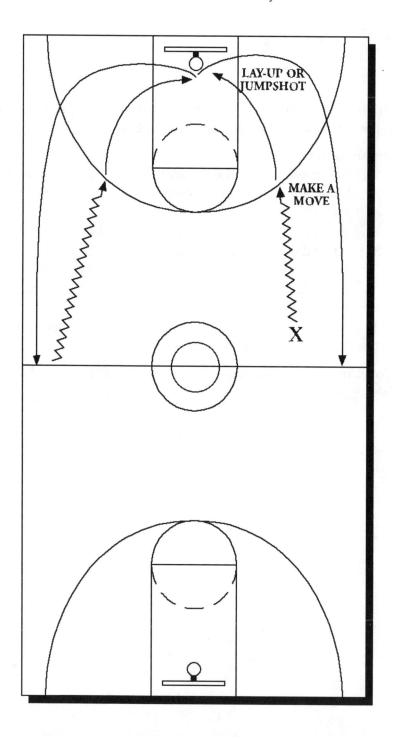

7 Spot Shooting

Coco Miller

Purpose: Improves conditioning and shooting ability. Also helps players to remain focused while tired.

Organization:
1. Begin with one shooter and one rebounder/passer.
2. Shooter begins in the corner at half court on either side and sprints to the first spot. Passer passes the ball to the shooter at the first spot and the shooter shoots.
3. After the shot is taken, shooter sprints to half court and back the second shooting spot. Meanwhile, the passer rebounds the ball and is ready to pass to the shooter at the second spot.
4. The drill continues until the shooter has taken a shot from each of the seven spots.

Coaching Notes: For variation, take one or two dribbles before each shot.

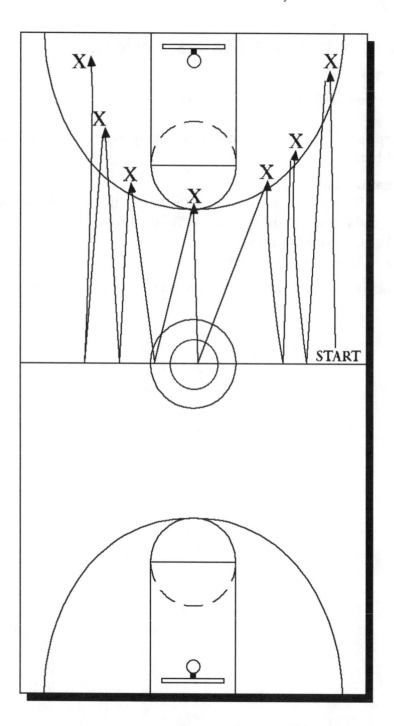

Proper Practice Makes Perfect: Jump Shots

From the Five-Star Basketball Archives

Purpose: Improve perimeter shooting with/without the dribble.

Organization:
1. Shoot 125 shots inside the three-point line, 125 outside the three-point line, and 100 free throws.
2. One dribble move.
3. More than one dribble, shot.

Coaching Notes: Make a goal each day for number of hits.

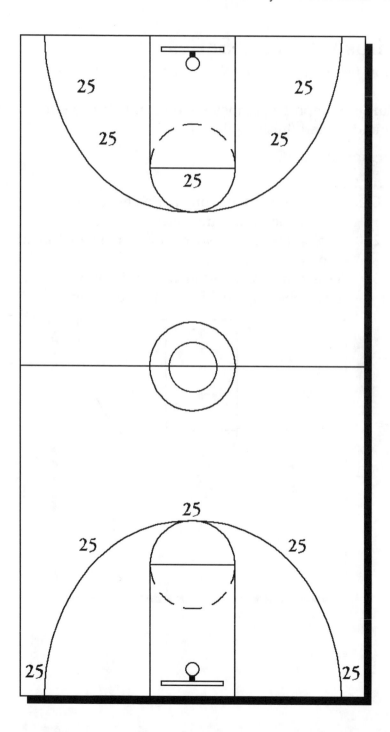

Finish the Play Series
From the Five-Star Basketball Archives

Purpose: Improve perimeter shooting. Improve offensive rebounding and finishing the shot.

Organization:

Drill One
Can be used to work on total perimeter game.
1. Players line up in three lines.
2. Players simultaneously go to execute two dribbles and shoot a jumper.
3. Players then rebound or rebound put back, and, with one dribble, pass the ball to the next man.

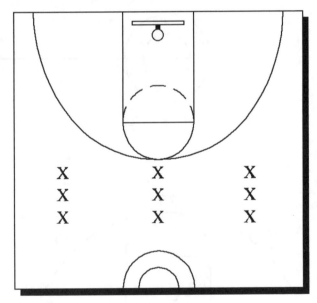

Drill Two

1. Two groups: one under basket, one on the perimeter.
2. Perimeter players speed dribble to a spot, assign area to go toward.
3. After five shots, rebounder and shooter switch.

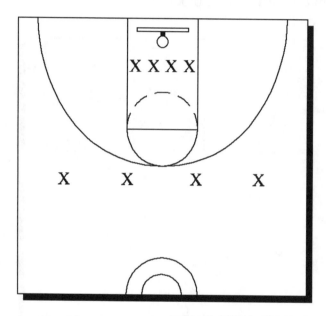

Drill Three

1. Two lines, each line has a ball.
2. First player in each line takes one/two dribbles to make an elbow jumper or other move (spin, crossover, etc.).
3. Work specifically on shot from "no-man's land" to get ball over big shot blocker

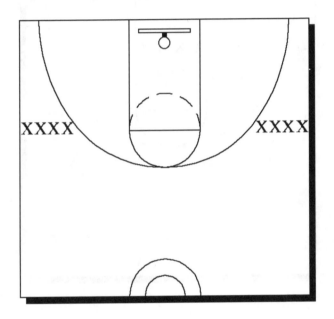

Five-Star campers learning how to use their own talents to be the best player they can be — the next Nikki could be practicing her ballhandling skills on our court

Learn to Play Like
Nikki McCray

"My heroes growing up were Michael Jordan and Flo-Jo (Florence Griffin Joyner) — they had and demanded respect," says Nikki McCray, a member of the 1996 and 2000 gold medal-winning Olympic teams and sixth all-time leading scorer in WNBA history.

Nikki's impressive basketball résumé started with the four SEC championships won by the Lady Vols during her tenure at Tennessee. She went on to be voted the most valuable player in the ABL in 1997 when she led the Columbus Quest to the ABL Championship. In 1998, she moved over to the WNBA Washington Mystics where she led in scoring (17.7 ppg, 4th in the WNBA), three-point shooting percentage (.315, 11th) and

Five-Star Quick Hitter

Nikki has tremendous ballhandling skills. She is particularly strong with the stop-and-go dribble and the hesitation dribble. To practice these skills, use the following Five-Star drills:

- ♦ Double Dribble, pages 86-87
- ♦ Game Condition Dribbling, pages 88-89
- ♦ Sideline to Sideline Moves, pages 96-97

assists (3.1 apg, 11th). She was voted a starter in the very first WNBA All-Stars game in 1999 and again in 2000.

Nikki, who color commentated for the Memphis Grizzlies during their first season in Memphis, considers moving without the ball her greatest strength as a player. "I would describe my game as very versatile, very athletic and very quick. Throughout my career I've developed into a person who can create, who can shoot the three."

To develop her shooting ability, Nikki says her favorite drill is simple: "Just shoot A LOT from five spots! Practice from off a pass and on a dribble."

"Nikki is a great defender and is always looking to get steals. She has the ability to shoot the three and take it to the basket, making her hard to guard as well," says Kelly Miller. "Nikki's competitive advantage shines through in her ability to think the game," according to Kristin Folkl. "She knows the game isn't over until the last whistle blows. And Katie Douglas says, "Nikki is polished. She's one of the best players in the league and is still getting better. She's got good size and strength for a guard. And her ability to hit the outside shot or penetrate makes her very tough to defend." Ukari Figgs adds, "Nikki is a smart player. She uses her experience to take advantage of picks and the defense that is being played against her."

Teammates from the Indiana Fever are also impressed with Nikki's play, "Nikki's creative moves and ability to shoot off the dribble are what make her such a great player. She didn't lead the ABL in scoring by luck, that's for sure!" says Tamika Catchings. "Nikki will try to help her teammates as much as she can. She hates to lose and it shows in the time she spends in preparation for competition."

> Nikki has a very quick first step and is also a terrific three-point shooter, which makes her hard to defend. She is also a great defender on or off the ball, always looking to get steals. — *Coco Miller*

Five-Star Quick Hitter

Nikki is also strong with the right and left pull-up shot. To practice this skill, do lots of shooting drills but also work on playing against tough opponents. To practice this, use the "Baseline to Midcourt Shooting Moves" drills on pages 98-100.

"Nikki's greatest strength as a player is her versatility," says Stephanie McCarty. "She is focused, determined and finds ways to win."

When asked to cite the coach who most influenced her, Nikki lists three: "Pat Summitt, Brian Agler and Tara VanDerveer. They want nothing but the best out of their players and challenged me all the time."

> She seems to really love the game ... very intense and can run for days!
> – *Nykesha Sales*

Nikki's advice for future all-stars: "Trust Jesus. Believe in yourself. Have fun."

Double Dribble

From the Five-Star Basketball Archives

Purpose: To improve ballhandling under pressure

Organization: Players line up at opposite ends of the top of key. They will meet face to face at halfcourt. Players must keep a low center of gravity and crossover shoulder to shoulder, hip to hip, while performing the following ballhandling skills. Dribble until players meet, then:

1. Execute a crossover dribble (right to left, left to right).
2. Crossover dribble through the legs.
3. Around the back dribble.
4. Control dribble to middle, two dribbles back and go, two dribbles back and crossover.
5. Different dribbles all around the court
   - Dribble with right hand, back and forth across line to half court center, come back using left hand.
   - Reverse spin dribble at corner. Execute a mini-jump-stop, reach with back leg to gain ground.
   - Stronghand dribble to middle, switch hands, back off two dribble and switch back to stronghand.
   - Fake reverse dribble (half-whirl), counter move against good cutting off defense.
   - Push it and pull it around back, around back dribble in corner and explode to the basket.
   - Stutter step, jab and crossover for drive to hold. Execute a left dribble setting up for stronghand crossover.

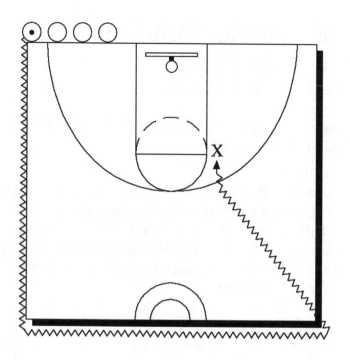

Game Condition Dribbling (Chair Style Optional)

From the Five-Star Basketball Archives

Purpose: To improve half-court and full-court ballhandling while simulating a defender.

Organization:

Start with offense players lined up on baseline. Offensive player executes a controlled dribble, protecting the ball, then retreat dribbles. Next, the player performs a crossover dribble to dribble up to the chair at half-court. The offensive player then dribbles through her legs, behind her back and power dribbles to the baseline.

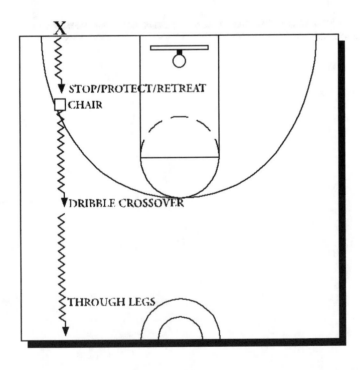

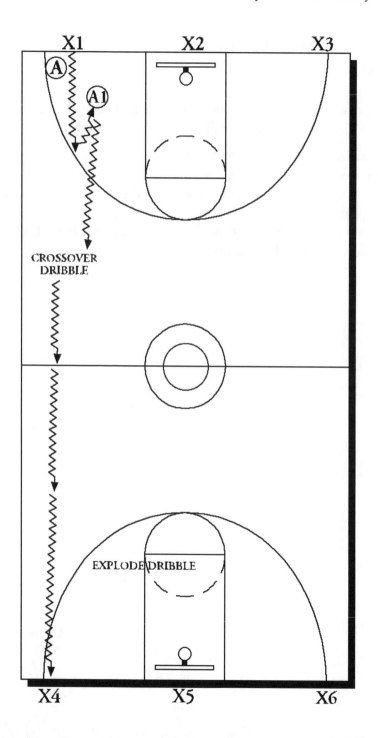

100 in Two Minutes

From the Five-Star Basketball Archives

Purpose: To improve such aspects of full-court transition offense as shooting, ballhandling and conditioning.

Organization: Players are divided into two equal groups. Both teams will try to total 100 points in two minutes (two points for a field goal, three points for a three-pointer) — deducting one point for every shot missed. Players must focus on passing, speed, dribbling, transition lay-ups from both the right and left sides and open floor jump shots.

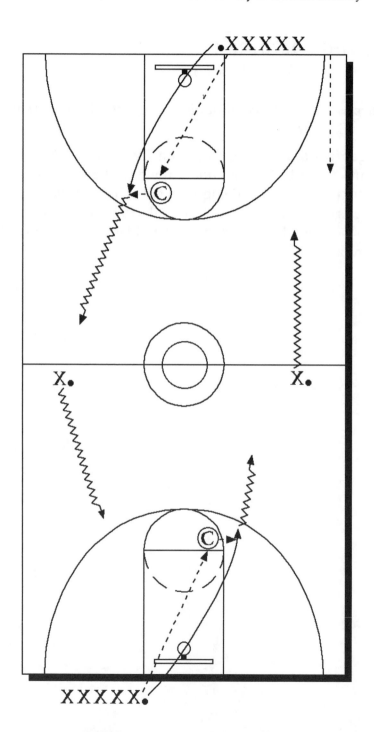

3-on-0 Fastbreak

From the Five-Star Basketball Archives

Purpose: Improve conditioning, game condition passing and transition offense.

Organization: Players are given five minutes to score 180 points. One player starts under the basket and passes the ball to the player who is going to shoot. The first player follows the pass while the shooter fastbreaks to the other end and follows her shot. Baseline runers do not leave until rebound has been taken.

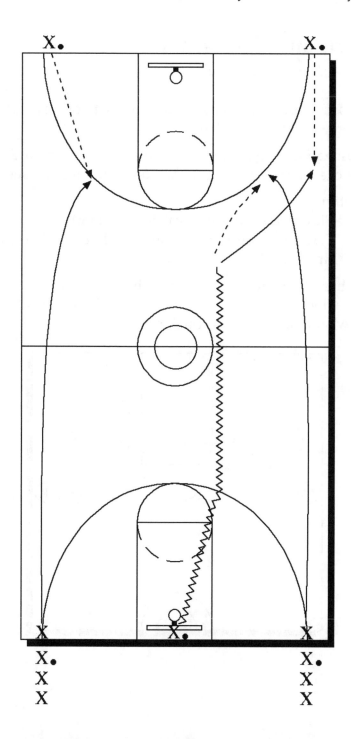

Catch and Concentrate

From the Five-Star Basketball Archives

Purpose: Improve player's endurance, footwork, catching and movement without the ball.

Organization: Player moves side-to-side for one minute, catching a chest pass, squaring to the hoop, but takes no shots.

Variations:
1. Player can take shots (catch and shoot).
2. Player can use a series of moves: shot fake, jab step and rip through.

Coaches Notes: If you are doing this correctly, you will get tired, which will help you learn how to shoot when fatigued and what adjustments you will need to make.

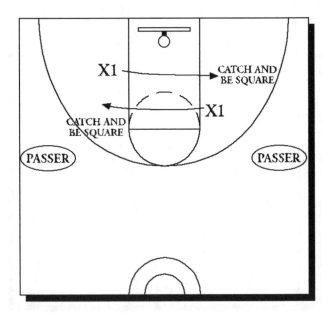

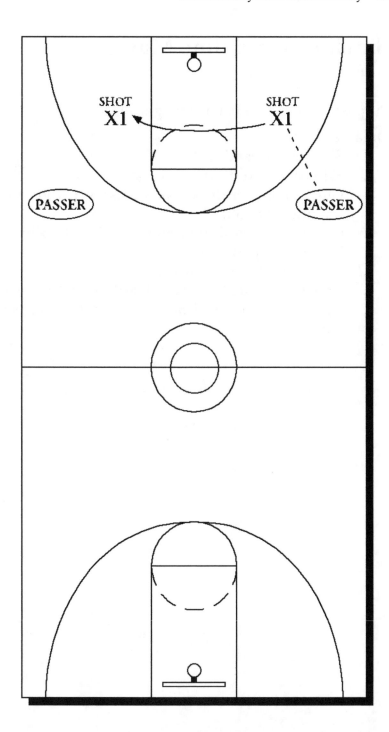

Sideline to Sideline Moves
From the Five-Star Basketball Archives

Purpose: To improve ballhandling skills.

Organization:
1. Skip forward and back.
2. Skip backward down and back.
3. Quick crossover dribble and crossover dribble (eyes up, dribbling tall).
4. Quick crossover dribble and pass the ball behind the back (eyes up, dribbling tall).
5. Mirror move, right to left.
6. Walk forward up the court while dribbling between the legs, coming back walk backward and dribbling behind the legs.

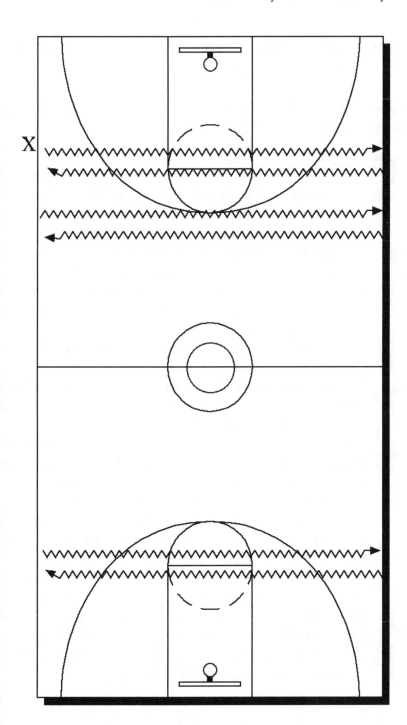

Baseline to Midcourt Shooting Moves
From the Five-Star Basketball Archives

Purpose: To develop a midrange shooting game by utilizing the dribble from the left and right sides of the floor.

Organization:
1. Left side to left side. Player starts at the left corner of the baseline and dribbles hard up the left sideline with the right hand. Once the player reaches half-court, she executes a behind the back spin dribble to the left hand. The ball is to be kept on the same side (left sideline) of the floor at all times. This is accomplished by performing a pivot and pull move. The player will plant (jump stop) at half-court, perform a forward pivot on her left foot while pulling the ball (placing the right hand in front of the ball) behind her back to the left side (left hand). Once she is facing straight ahead, she is to take two hard dribbles with the left hand and pull up for a jump stop at the left baseline. Reverse this to practice right side to right side.

2. Left side to right side. Same as the above movement, except that the player will start on the baseline in the short-corner area. When the player reaches halfcourt, she will execute the same hand dribble move by performing a pivot and pull move. She will jump stop at half-court, perform a forward pivot on her left foot while pulling the ball (placing the right hand in front of the ball) behind her back with her right hand at the center of her body and quickly grab it again with her right hand. Once she is facing straight ahead, she will take two hard dribbles with her right hand and pull up for a jump shot in the middle of the free-throw line. Reverse this to practice right side to left side.

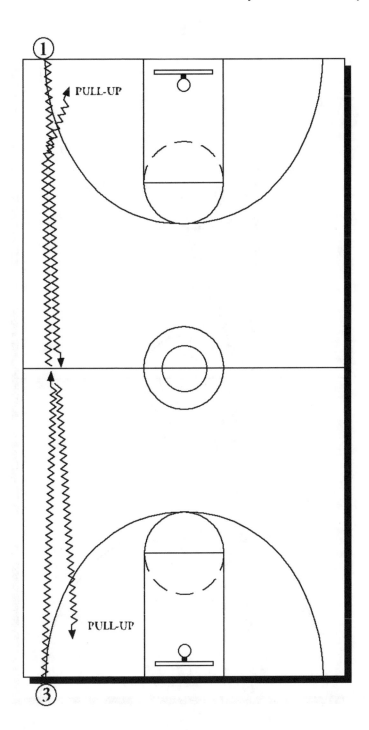

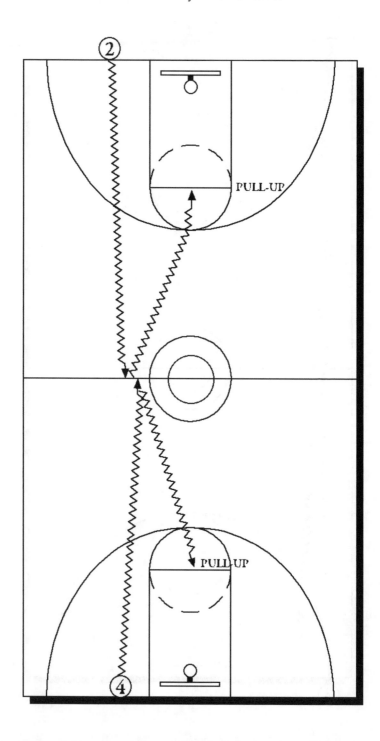

Nikki McCray can stop-and-go, hesitate with the dribble, stop on dime and pull-up for her jumper — skills you can learn, too

**Coming off and utilizing the screen to set up the
pick and roll, Ukari Figgs-style**

Learn to Play Like
Ukari Figgs

"I think my greatest strength as a player is my jump shot. I am a consistent jump shooter because I work hard in the off season on my shooting and my footwork."

"She's a terrific shooter," agrees Coco Miller, "but she can also penetrate and finish, which makes her hard to defend." Tamika Catchings differs somewhat from their viewpoint, "Ukari's great strength is her ability to create as a point guard. She can handle the ball and knows how to deliver it to her teammates." Stephanie McCarty agrees, "She has the ability to get the ball to her team-mates in a position to be successful."

"Ukari is a solid point guard, gets her team involved and controls her team," says Tina Thompson. "She is an offensive threat — you can't give her open looks at the basket because she'll make you pay."

Not all areas of the game have been come easily to Ukari, she admits "I've had to work hard to improve my ability to drive to the basket and finish. I've played a lot of pick-up games and worked a great deal on ballhandling skills." Her favorite drills include shooting from side-to-side, starting at the baseline and finishing up top and full-court jumpers and moves.

Her hard work shows when she takes to the court, and her love of the game is just as apparent. "Ukari enjoys the challenges competition provides," says Kristin Folkl. Catchings echoes this sentiment, "Ukari is a fierce competitor that inspires her teammates to follow along with her when she gets riled. She is the kind of player anyone

U kari is a great playmaker and a very nice defender.
— *Nykesha Sales*

would love to have on their team." Nikki McCray adds, "She handles adverse situations well — she led the Sparks to a championship at a very young age!"

"I do love the game," says Ukari. I've been playing organized ball since I was six." As a young player, she looked up to Dawn Staley and Cheryl Miller, "Great college players! I admired the way they lead their respective teams to victory."

Ukari also admires Carolyn Peck, "She is a motivator and listens to her players. She is down-to-earth and makes practice and playing for her fun. She doesn't yell, and she is never negative."

Her admiration for Coach Peck stems from her playing days at Purdue, where she was the 14th player in school history to score 1000 points. Ukari was part of Peck's 1999 squad that won the NCAA Championship. As a matter of fact, she was selected as the Most Outstanding Player at the 1999 NCAA Final Four.

Ukari says the keys to success are simple:
1) Work hard.
2) Never let anyone tell you what you cannot do.
3) Never be satisfied with yourself as a player. There are always areas to be worked on.

Five-Star Quick Hitter

Ukari works hard to create situations for her teammates — how do you work to get your teammates open? Five-Star drills that will help your team work for the best shot include the "Up-Screen Game" on page 113 and the "Dribbling and Passing Games on page 114-115.

Game Situation Jumpers (120 made 2's)

From the Five-Star Basketball Archives

Purpose: To improve shooting under game-like conditions.

Organization: Use a Shoot-A-Way to make ball recovery more simple.

1. Shoot 45-degree bank shots (make 40).
   a. Catch and shoot with proper form, ball should be shot higher than the square and hit glass on the downward flight.
   b. Make 20 from each side.
2. Swing shot, take off rack (make 20).
   a. Square on inside foot, jump 6 inches forward.
   b. One-second follow-through.
3. One-dribble pull-up, bounce pass off rack (make 20).
   a. Jump stop, shot fake, push off.
   b. Alternate right and left.
4. WNBA curl, elbow screen fade (make 20 each side).

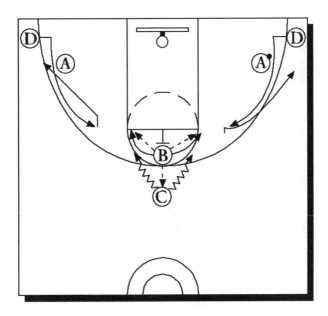

14 Spot Shooting
Ukari Figgs

Purpose: Improves perimeter shooting and offensive rebounding.

Organization:
1. Begin by designating 14 shooting spots along the three-point line or within a player's range.
2. Player shoots from spot one and gets her own rebound.
3. Player runs to spot two, shoots, gets her own rebounds and returns to spot one.
4. After the player has made five shots from both spots, she moves to spot three.
5. Player shoots from spot three, gets her own rebound and runs to spot four. After the player has made five shots from spots three and four, she moves to spot five.
6. Drill continues until the player has made five shots from each spot.

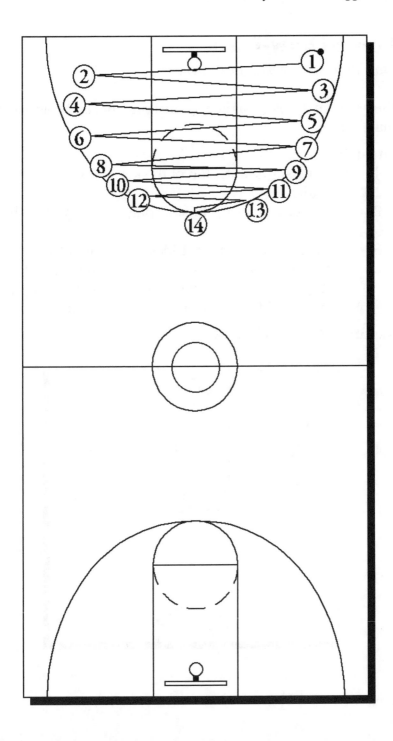

Drive-Draw-Dish
From the Five-Star Basketball Archives

Purpose: To develop passing against pressure and help a team-mate score.

Organization:
1. Player 1 starts at the top of the key and penetrates past defender 1.
2. Defender 2 steps up to stop player 1 in the middle of the lane.
3. Player 1 jump stops and kicks a one-handed (outside hand) the pass to player 2, who is spotting up for the shot. (If on the right side, then the one-handed pass is with the right hand away from the defender.)

Variation: Go to both sides.

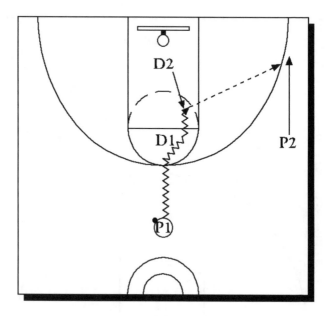

Game Situation Jumpers (200 made 3's)

From the Five-Star Basketball Archives

Purpose: To enhance and improve mid-range shooting.

Organization: Use a Shoot-A-Way to make ball recovery more simple.

1. Make 50 from each side of rack from two different areas.
2. Change area of racks each day
   a. Post players make 25 off each side of rack, 100 total. Then shoot 25 jump hooks, 25 turn-arounds each side of shoot-a-way.

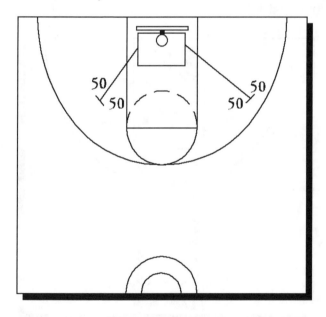

Up and Downs with One Ball

From the Five-Star Basketball Archives

Purpose: Improves both strong- and weak-hand ballhanding.

Organization:
1. Player dribbles length of floor with strong hand, then weak hand.
2. A cycle is one trip baseline-to-baseline.
3. Concentrate on looking at the time.
4. This is a warm-up, therefore the player can jog.
5. Shoot weak hand lay-ups on each cycle (2 reverses, 2 strong side).

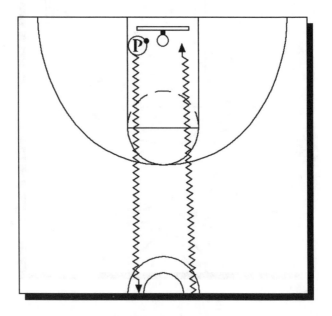

Up and Downs with Two Balls

From the Five-Star Basketball Archives

Purpose: To develop strong- and weak-hand ballhandling.

Organization:
1. Same as previous drill except player has two balls.
2. Players can add a zig-zag motion in this drill.
3. Can also add all dribbles as well (stutter, behind the back, etc.).
4. Pick up the pace to 75% on this drill.

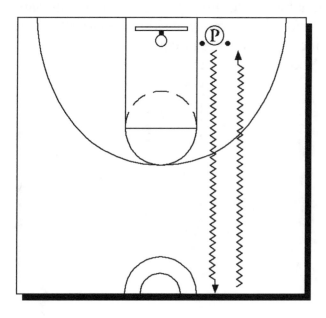

Dribble Moves with Lay-up Finish

From the Five-Star Basketball Archives

Purpose: To improve speed and shooting while attacking and utilizing the dribble to the basket.

Organization:
1. Attack basket at full speed at arc area, execute move, then one-dribble to finish.
2. Use all lay-up techniques (straight, inside hand, reverse, baby hook, two-feet power lay-up, etc.).
3. Dribble out to next spot using same with same hand.
4. Perform same move at side of circle, other side of circle and opposite side of court.
5. Procced to next move.

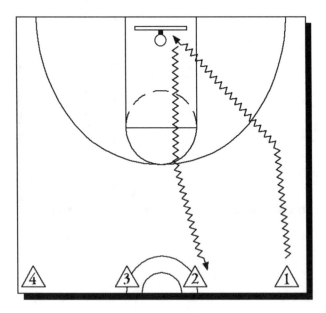

Up-Screen Game

From the Five-Star Basketball Archives

Purpose: To develop screening techniques, getting open for the shot and assisting a teammate.

Organization:
1. Player simulates a back pick (screen) on the first cone and steps to catch a pass and shoot the jump shot.
2. Player back picks, steps to catch, makes a quick-decision drive toward the second cone and makes a jump shot.
3. Player catches the ball, makes a quick decision drive, executes a change of direction dribble at both the second and third cones, then finishes with a reverse lay-in or a baby hook shot.

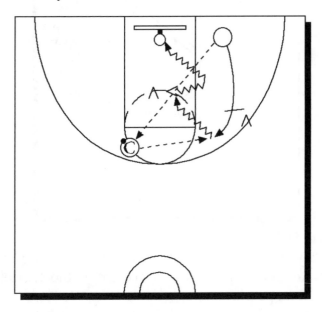

Dribbling and Passing Games
From the Five-Star Basketball Archives

Purpose: To develop game conditioning dribbling and passing skills.

Part One: Look In
1. Player 1 dribbles around the three-point line, looking to player 2 in the post.
2. Player 1 changes hands as he changes direction from right to left to right.

Variation: Add a player to the middle as a target and when the pass is made to the target, the passer yells, "Shot."

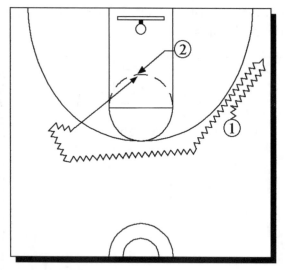

Part Two: Drive and Turn
1. Player 1 dribbles from the left corner with the left hand.
2. Defender 1 rotates over from the right block to left block and stops player 1.
3. Player 1 picks up his dribble and turns out (pivots) toward the baseline.
4. Player 1 then passes to the next player in line.

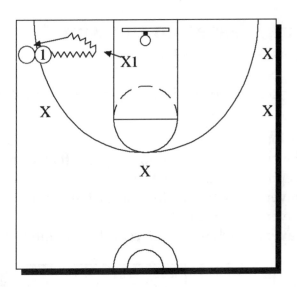

Variation: Can be done from all "X" spots.

Part Three: Run Around

1. Player 1 is located in the lane.
2. Player 2 runs around the key and practices catching any pass by getting behind the ball.

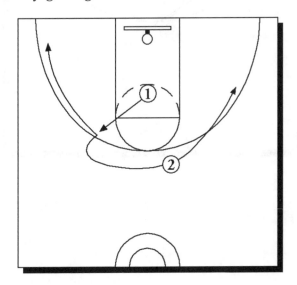

Catching Passes on the Run

From the Five-Star Basketball Archives

Purpose: To develop conditioning, catching and shooting on the run.

Organization:
1. Player 1 runs back and forth from left block to left wing keeping her outside hand up.
2. Player 2 has ball at the top of the key and passes to player 1 and yells, "Shot."
3. Player 1 catches the ball and shoots immediately.

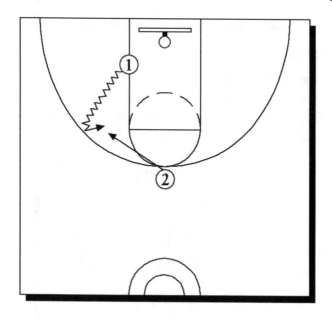

Catching and Scoring

From the Five-Star Basketball Archives

Purpose: To develop conditioning, catching and shooting skills in transition.

Organization:
1. Players start at half-court and runs up ahead of the pass.
2. Player 1 passes to players on the run.
3. Players catch and go to the basket or pull up for jump shot in transition. Practice on both sides.

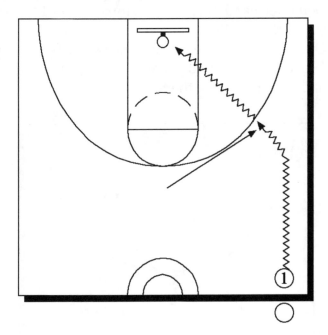

Defense: Drawing the Double

From the Five-Star Basketball Archives

Purpose: To develop ballhandling against pressure. To initiate offensive transition by passing to an open teammate.

Organization:
1. Player 1 starts directly under the basket.
2. Player 1 beats defender 1 and defender 2 down the floor off the dribble.
3. Defender 1 and 2 retreat to stop player 1.
4. Defender 1 and 2 converge to force player 1 from breaking to the sideline.
5. Once stopped at the sideline and before trapped, player 1 reverses the ball to player 2 or kicks up to player 3 at halfcourt to initiate the fast break.

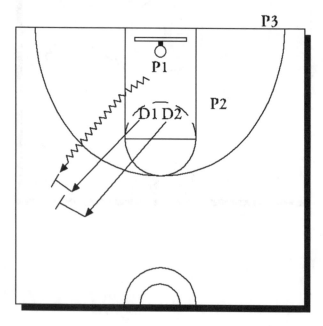

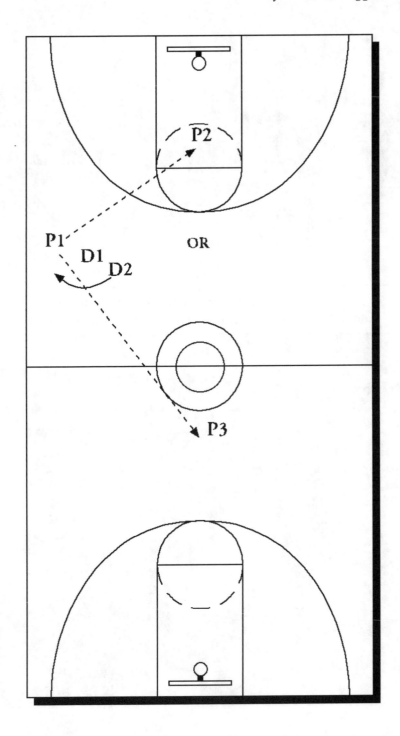

Pushing it up the floor: Five-Star teaches transition offense
and ambidextrous ballhandling skills, à la Stephanie McCarty

Learn to Play Like
Stephanie McCarty

Stephanie White McCarty is one of the legendary figures of Indiana basketball. Stephanie is Indiana's career scoring leader in girls basketball with 2,869 points; her season scoring totals of 886 (her senior year of high school) and 838 (her junior year of high school) rank second and third on the state's season scoring chart. She was voted Indiana Miss Basketball in 1995 and then went on to Purdue University to play college basketball.

The winner of the 1999 Wade Trophy and runner up for National Player of the Year, Stephanie was named 1998-1999 First Team All-American for leading Purdue to their first-ever NCAA Championship by the AP, Kodak, *Sports Illustrated*, *The Sporting News*, USBWA and *Women's Basketball Journal*. She started her professional basketball career during the 1999 season with the Charlotte Sting but then returned to Indiana when the Fever started playing in the summer of 2000. She sat out the 2002 season with an injury, but is hoping to return for 2003.

Five-Star Quick Hitter

Women's camp director Matt Masiero once saw Stephanie score over 30 points twice in the same day as a junior in high school during the Indiana State Girls' Tournament. "She came in and dominated in the morning session and then returned later to do the same on both ends of the floor. She was truly one of the toughest competitors I have ever seen — man or woman."

When asked what she would most like to be known for as a player, Stephanie replied, "I will do whatever I can to help my team succeed, whether that be on the floor, in practice or cheering from the bench — anything that will help to better our team. Role players are vital to a team's success.

"I think my greatest strength is my knowledge of the game and ability to coach on the floor. I study game tapes of many players and continue to learn from other players and coaches."

Katie Douglas (who counts Stephanie among her role models in the game) says, "Stephanie's greatest strength is her understanding of the game. I've had the privilege to watch her and play with her, so I know first-hand that her knowledge is second-to-none." Steph's not the quickest or the most athletic player, but her court awareness is unmatched." Tamika Catchings says of Stephanie, "She's a smart player that has studied the game. She may not be the quickest person on the court, but she finds other ways to contribute."

You can tell Steph has a strong desire to win. She's a leader whose passion for the game carries over to her teammates. – *Kelly Miller*

Stephanie, unlike many athletes, does not claim an athlete as her role model. "Neil Armstrong (the first man to walk on the moon) was my hero when I was growing up. He did something no one had ever done before, and that seemed to me to make dreams seem attainable for anyone."

Other influences include her high school coach, Tom Polf of Seeger High School. "Coach Polf taught me how to be patient and let things come to me. He also knows the game better than any other coach I have had."

Stephanie's skills came as the result of hours of long practice, "I used to get up about 5:30 in the morning and have breakfast with my grandpa," Stephanie was quoted as saying in an article in the *Times-Union* newspaper. "Then he would take me to the gym by 6:00 a.m. so I could workout and shoot around. Then I would go to class and practice. After I got home, I would do my homework and then go outside to play basketball some more. I could never get enough basketball. It's my passion, my desire."

Stephanie's favorite drills include the 11-Man Break, "because you get conditioning along with competition and can work on fast break opportunities." (See page 124-125 for this drill). She also likes to practice two ball dribbling with her eyes open and closed.

The area of her game that she feels required the most work was taking the ball to the basket with a one-on-one move. To improve this area, Steph says she "... played a lot of one-on-one with guys and worked on moves with no defense."

When asked what her advice for up-and-coming players would be, Stephanie offers the following:

> On or off the court, Steph is giving it her all.
> – *Tamika Catchings*

"First, Education is the most important thing. No one can ever take that away from you. Second, anything is possible as long as you are willing to sacrifice and work hard to accomplish your goals. And finally, your character will take you much farther in life than anything else you could ever do.

11 Man Break

Stephanie McCarty

Purpose: To simulate and enhance the transition offense with a drill that makes players concentrate on passing and running the floor. This drill also improves defensive skills.

Organization:
1. The drill begins with three offensive players attacking two defensive players in a 3-on-2 formation.
2. The defender that gets the rebound or makes a basket passes the ball to one of the two outlets at half court.
3. The passer and both outlets continue the drill on the other end of the court.

Coaching Notes:
- Make sure the offensive players stay spread out beyond the wing to begin the transition offense.
- Make sure players focus on pushing the ball hard, making sharp passes and looking for the open lay-up.

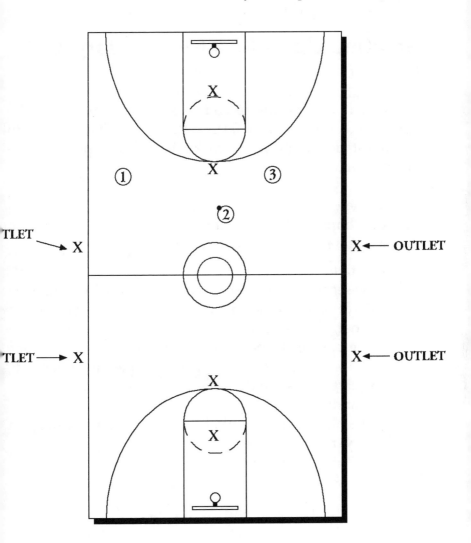

Spotting Up — Be a Moving Target!

From the Five-Star Basketball Archives

When you pass inside you must move — make the defender find you and move farther. Remember that it is easy to guard a stationary player, so make the defender pay for doubling down.

Game One

Purpose: Improves passing and relocation for the shot after the pass and movement without the ball.

Organization:

1. Passer feeds the post player from the wing. The post player catches the ball and is in basketball position to shoot, pass or dribble.
2. The post feeds the wing who has faded to the corner. The wing catches a chest pass in triple threat position, squares her shoulders and is ready to shoot.
3. Post player yells, "Shot."
4. The players rotate, with the shooter becoming the post player.

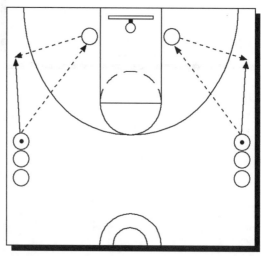

Game Two

Purpose: Moving without the ball and becoming hard to guard.

Organization:

1. Point passes to highpost on elbow for hand-off pass.
2. Wing player v-cuts to overtop for flip and three-pointer. Wing must square shoulders (pivot off inside foot, swing gate with outside).
3. Players rotate with first cutter becoming the wing player, second cutter becoming the post player and the post going to the end of the line for point guards.

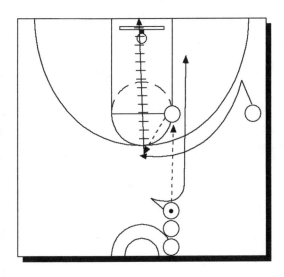

Six Ambidextrous Basketball Games
From the Five-Star Basketball Archives

Purpose: To develop shooting and ballhandling with the right and left hand.

Game One: 50 Spot Form Shooting

Organization:
1. Shoot three-foot, three spot jumpers (10 times shot) with proper grip, shot pocket, rotation and followthrough, and footwork.
2. Shoot elbow jumpers (10 times each elbow).

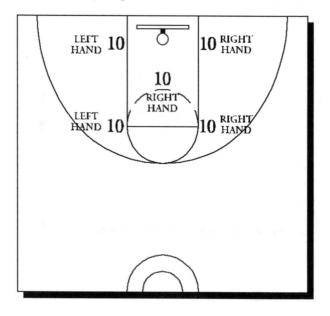

Game Two: Game Situation Jumpers – 120 made 2's

Organization:

1. Shoot 45-degree banks, make 40. Catch and shoot as in game one. Ball should be shot higher than square and hit glass on downward flight. 20 each side.
2. Swing shot, take off rack, make 20. Square on inside foot. Jump six inches forward. One-second followthrough.
3. One dribble pull-up (bounce pass off rack), make 20. Jump stop, shot fake, push off. Alternate right and left.
4. WNBA curl, elbow screen fade, make 20 each side. Use passer or take off rack and toss to self.

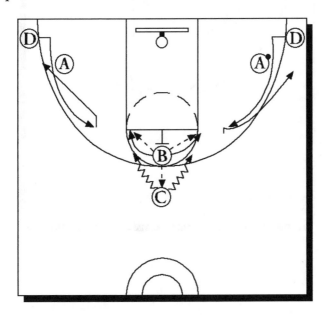

Game Three: Game Situation Jumpers — 200 made 3's

Organization:

1. Make 50 from each side of rack from two different areas.

2. Post players make 25 off each side of rack, 100 total. Then shoot 25 jump hooks and 25 turn-a-rounds on each side of the shoot away.

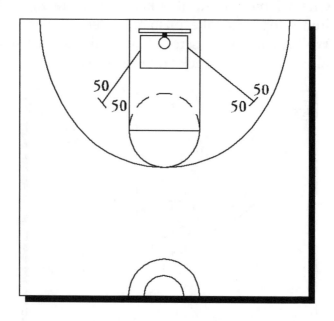

Game Four: Up and Downs — One Ball

Organization:
1. Player dribbles length of floor with strong hand then weak hand.
2. A cycle is one trip baseline to baseline.
3. Concentrate on looking at the rim.
4. This is a warm-up, therefore the player can jog.
5. Shoot weakhand lay-ups on each cycle (two reverses, two strongside).

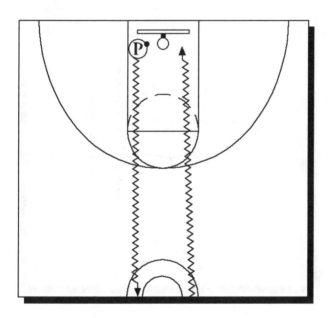

Game Five: Up and Downs — Two Balls (see diagram top of next page)

Organization:

1. Same as the previous drill except player has two balls.
2. Players can add a zig-zag motion in this drill.
3. Can also add all dribbles as well (for example, stutter, behind the back, etc.).
4. Pick up pace to 75% on this drill.

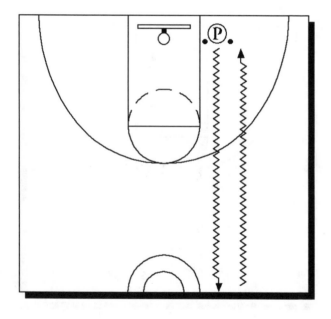

Game Six: Dribble Moves with Lay-up Finish

Organization:

1. Attack basket at full speed at arc area, execute move then dribble to finish.
2. Use all lay-up techniques (for example, straight, inside hand, reverse, baby-hook, two-feet power lay-up, etc.).
3. Dribble out to next spot using same with same hand.
4. Perform same move at side of circle, other side of circle, opposite side of the court. Proceed to the next move.

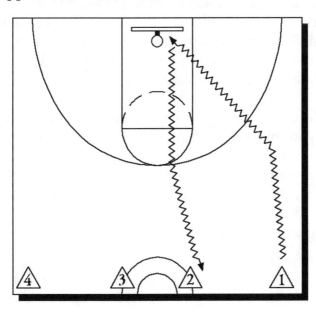

Appendix:
In-Season Strength and Conditioning

Matt Brzycki, Coordinator of Recreational Fitness and Wellness Programs, Princeton University

Several years ago, I was asked by the athletic director of a college to speak to all of the coaches in his department about strength and conditioning. At one point, I was discussing the basic elements of in-season training when the women's basketball coach told me that she simply wanted her athletes to "maintain" their strength during the season. My response was: "No offense, coach, but why would you want them to maintain their strength during the season when they could improve it?"

Indeed, it is during the competitive season that you need to be at your highest levels of strength and conditioning. That being said, the goal of the in-season program should be to optimize your level of strength and conditioning. (Keep in mind, too, that the concepts for in-season training apply to *any* time throughout the year when you compete such as summer leagues/tournaments.)

Program Specifics

For the most part, the training that you do when you are in-season should virtually mirror the training that you do when you are not in-season with the main difference being a reduction in the amount of time that you devote to strength and conditioning activities. The following is a brief description of program specifics for strength training and conditioning done during the season:

Strength Training

If a muscle does not receive appropriate stimulation within a certain number of days, it will progressively lose strength. That is why it is important for you to continue strength training on a regular basis even when you are in-season. Regardless of the type of approach that you implement for strength training and conditioning, most of the program variables should remain the same — or nearly the same — during the season. These include the level of effort with which you lift weights, the way in which you systematically progress in resistance, the number of repetitions that you perform for each exercise, the manner in which you raise and lower the resistance, the order in which you do the exercises and the way in which you record your training data.

Here are the remaining program variables that demand some degree of modification or consideration when you are in-season:

1. The number of sets of each exercise. Whether or not you are in-season, you should do the minimum number of sets necessary to produce an adequate level of muscular fatigue. During the season is not the time to increase the number of sets in your workout. If you do three sets of each exercise when you are not in-season, think about reducing this number when you are in-season.

2. The duration of the workout. When not in-season, you should complete your strength training in less than about one hour per session; during the season, the length of your workouts should not exceed about 30 minutes per session.

3. The number of exercises in each workout. When you are not in-season, you can perform a comprehensive strength-training workout for basketball using no more than about 15 exercises (assuming a total-body workout). The focal point for most of these exercises should be your major muscle groups — namely, your hips, legs and upper torso. During the season, you should reduce your volume of exercises. Here, your strength-training

routine can consist of as few as seven exercises that
address the major muscles of your body. Figure 1 offers two sample in-season workouts that you can do on
an alternating basis.

4.   The frequency of training. When not in-season, it is sug-
gested that you perform your strength training two–
three times per week on nonconsecutive days such as
on Monday and Thursday or Monday, Wednesday and
Friday. During the season, however, the increased en-
ergy demands of practices and games and even travel
require you to decrease the frequency of your training.
In order to provide greater recovery when in-season,
then, the frequency of your strength training should be
reduced to one–two times per week. In this case, you
should lift as soon as possible following your game
and not within about 48 hours of your next game. So if
you play on Saturday and Tuesday, you should lift on
Sunday and Wednesday (or Thursday — providing that
it is not within about 48 hours of your next game). From
time to time, you may only be able to lift weights once
a week because of a particularly heavy schedule such
as playing three games in one week, participating in a
holiday or post-season tournament and so on.

Conditioning

Once the season begins, most of your conditioning work
can be done during practice time. This can be accomplished
by simply running up and down the court as part of practice
whether it be participating in game-like situations or doing
skill-related drills. Sometimes you can do traditional sprints,
covering various distances either during or at the end of practice.

NOTE: *This chapter represents a thumbnail sketch of in-season strength and conditioning
for basketball. A more detailed description of overall training can be found in the book*
Conditioning for Basketball *written by Matt Brzycki and Shaun Brown (the strength
and conditioning coach of the Boston Celtics).*

WORKOUT #1	WORKOUT #2
Leg Press	Leg Curl
Leg Extension	Bench Press
Seated Row/Bent-Over Row	Overhead Press
Abdominal Crunch/Sit-up	Hip Abduction
Hip Adduction	Calf Raise/Dorsi Flexion
Incline Press	Lat Pulldown
Upright Row	Side Bend/Rotary Torso

Figure 1: Two Sample In-Season Workouts

The Bottom Line

Understand that you should do strength training and conditioning on a year-round basis — including the basketball season. If you worked hard during the off-season and pre-season to improve your levels of strength and conditioning, it makes little sense to terminate these activities when the most important part of your year begins. Finally, there is no need to make dramatic changes in your program once you launch into your season. In general, you simply need to reduce the amount of time that you dedicate to strength training and conditioning.

Five-Star Contributors

Scott Adubato (Five-Star Quick Hitters) played for Division III powerhouse Upsala College in upstate NY. He was an assistant coach at Georgia State. He has been a Five-Star coach, lecturer and station master for 15 years

Matt Brzycki is the Coordinator of Recreational Fitness and Wellness Programs at Princeton University. He is the author of five books (including *A Practical Approach to Strength Training*) and the editor of *Maximize Your Training* (a 455-page book that features chapters written by 37 strength and fitness professionals). Brzycki also co-authored the book *Conditioning for Basketball* with Shaun Brown, the strength and conditioning coach of the Boston Celtics. He is also the author of more than 215 articles on strength and fitness for 36 different publications.

On behalf of **Leigh Klein**, President, Five-Star Basketball Camp and Coach **Matt Masiero**, Director, Five-Star Women's Basketball Camp, we would like to thank the countless coaches, who for the past four decades have contributed to the premier teaching camp in the country. They have supplied numerous drills that have been utilized in successful basketball programs all over country and handed down from each generation. Each coach has also provided hours of dedication and instruction, and is the sole reason that Five-Star Basketball Camp is "Where the teaching never stops!" Thank you for your effort and support! Our thanks also goes to Five-Star staffers Tony Bergeron, Keith Holubesko, Jessica Mannetti, Kevin Pigott and Matthew Weiss.

We would also like to thank Lon Babby, Jim Tanner, Jason Levien and Shana Martin of the law firm of Williams and Connolly, LLP for their help in bringing this project to completion.

A week at Five-Star showcases the two determining factors in your basketball success: the desire to learn and the love of the game